Life Without Conflict

- Dada Bhagwan

Editor : Dr. Niruben Amin

Publisher : Mr. Ajit C. Patel
Dada Bhagwan Aradhana Trust
Dada Darshan, 5, Mamta Park Soc,
B/h. Navgujrat College, Usmanpura,
Ahmedabad-380014,
Gujarat, India.
Tel. : +91 79 3983 0100

First Edition : 2000 copies, March 2006
Second Edition : 2000 copies, June 2007
Third Edition : 2000 copies, March 2010
Fourth Edition : 2000 copies, January 2014

Price : Ultimate Humility (leads to Universal oneness)
and Awareness of "I Don't Know Anything"

Rs. 40.00

Printer : Amba Offset
Basement, Parshwanath Chambers,
Nr. RBI, Usmanpura,
Ahmedabad-380014, Gujarat, India.
Tel. : +91 79 27542964

Trimantra

The Three Mantras that Destroy All Obstacles in Life

Namo Vitaragaya
I bow to the One who is absolutely free from all attachment and abhorrence

Namo Arihantanam
I bow to the living One who has annihilated all internal enemies of anger, pride, deceit and greed

Namo Siddhanam
I bow to the Ones who have attained the state of total and final liberation

Namo Aayariyanam
I bow to the Self-realized masters who impart knowledge of liberation to others

Namo Uvazzayanam
I bow to those who have received the Knowledge of the Self and are helping others attain the same

Namo Loye Savva Sahunam
I bow to all saints everywhere who have received the Knowledge of the Self

Eso Pancha Namukkaro
These five salutations

Savva Pavappanasano
Destroy all demerit karma

Mangalanam cha Savvesim
Of all that is auspicious

Padhamam Havai Mangalam
This is the highest

Om Namo Bhagavate Vasudevaya
I bow to all who have attained the absolute Self in human form

Om Namah Shivaya
I bow to all human beings who have become instruments for salvation of the world

Jai Sat Chit Anand
Awareness of the Eternal is Bliss

Books of Akram Vignan of Dada Bhagwan

1. Adjust Everywhere
2. Ahimsa : Non-Violence
3. Anger
4. Aptavani - 1
5. Aptavani - 2
6. Aptavani - 4
7. Aptavani - 5
8. Aptavani - 6
9. Aptavani - 8
10. Aptavani - 9
11. Autobiography of Gnani Purush A.M.Patel
12. Avoid Clashes
13. Brahmacharya : Celibacy Attained With Understanding
14. Death : Before, During & After...
15. Flawless Vision
16. Generation Gap
17. Harmony In Marriage
18. Life Without Conflict
19. Money
20. Noble Use of Money
21. Pratikraman : The master key that resolves all conflicts (Abridge & Big Volume)
22. Pure Love
23. Right Understanding to Help Others
24. Science of Karma
25. Science of Speech
26. Shree Simandhar Swami : The Living God
27. The Essence Of All Religion
28. The Fault Is Of the Sufferer
29. The Guru and The Disciple
30. Tri Mantra : The mantra that removes all worldly obstacles
31. Whatever Happened is Justice
32. Who Am I ?
33. Worries

'Dadavani' Magazine is published Every month

Note About This Translation

Gnani Purush Ambalal M. Patel, popularly known as Dadashri or Dada or Dadaji, used to say that it is not possible to exactly translate his satsang on the Science of Self-Realization and the art of worldly interaction, into English. Some of the depth and intent of meaning to be conveyed to the seeker, would be lost. He stressed the importance of learning Gujarati to precisely understand all his teachings.

Dadashri did however grant his blessings to convey his original words to the world through translations in English and other languages. It was his deepest desire and fervor that the suffering human beings of the world attain the living freedom of the wonderful Akram Vignan that expressed within him. He further stated that a day would come when the world would be in awe of the phenomenal powers of this science.

This is an humble attempt to present to the world the essence of the teachings of Dadashri, the Gnani Purush. A lot of care has been taken to preserve the tone and message of his words. This is not a literal translation of his words. Many individuals have worked diligently for this product and we remain deeply thankful to them all.

This is an elementary introduction to the vast new treasure of his teachings. Please note that any errors committed in the translation are entirely those of the translators and for those we request your pardon.

The World Has Been Given
Religion & Knowledge of Worldly Interaction

Make a book that has the knowledge of worldly interactions. If people's worldly interactions improve it would be enough. These words of mine will change their minds for the benefit of all. Keep my words as they are. Do not alter them. They have tremendous power in them. They are without any sense of ownership. The preparation for publication and presentation is your task.

This knowledge of mine on the art and science of worldly interaction is such that it will be useful for all in the world. The entire mankind will benefit from it.

My worldly interaction was very ideal. I am teaching worldly interaction as well as religion. Everyone will benefit, from the one with gross understanding to the one with subtle understanding. Therefore do something that will help all people. I have read many books that claim to help the world, but they fall short. They may help a little, but none exist that make a meaningful improvement in life. For this you need a doctor of the mind. I am the absolute doctor of mind.

~Dadashri

Introduction to The 'Gnani Purush'

On a June evening in 1958 at around six o'clock, Ambalal Muljibhai Patel, a family man, a contractor by profession, was sitting on a bench on the busy platform number 3 of Surat's train station. Surat is a city in south Gujarat, a western state in India. What happened within the next forty-eight minutes was phenomenal. Spontaneous Self-realization occurred within Ambalal M. Patel. During this event his ego completely melted and from that moment onwards he became completely detached from all Ambalal's thoughts, speech and acts. He became the Lord's living instrument for the salvation of mankind, through the path of knowledge. He called this Lord, Dada Bhagwan. To everyone he met, he would say, "This Lord, Dada Bhagwan is fully manifest within me. He also resides within all living beings. The difference is that within me He is completely expressed and in you, he is yet to manifest."

Who are we? What is God? Who runs this world? What is karma? What is liberation? Etc. All the world's spiritual questions were answered during this event. Thus nature offered absolute vision to the world through the medium of Shree Ambalal Muljibhai Patel.

Ambalal was born in Tarsali, a suburb of the city of Baroda and raised in Bhadran, Gujarat. His wife's name was Hiraba. Although he was a contractor by profession, his life at home and his interaction with everyone around him was exemplary even prior to his Self-realization. After becoming Self-realized and attaining the state of a Gnani, (The Awakened One), his body became a 'public charitable trust.'

Throughout his whole life he lived by the principle that there should not be any commerce in religion, and in all commerce there must be religion. He also never took money

7

from anyone for his own use. He used the profits from his business to take his devotees for pilgrimages to various parts of India.

His words became the foundation for the new, direct and step-less path to Self-realization called Akram Vignan. Through his divine original scientific experiment (The Gnan Vidhi), he imparted this knowledge to others within two hours. Thousands have received his grace through this process and thousands continue to do so even now. 'Akram' means without steps; an elevator path or a short cut, whereas 'Kram' means an orderly step-by-step spiritual path. Akram is now recognized as a direct shortcut to the bliss of the Self.

Who is Dada Bhagwan ?

When he explained to others who 'Dada Bhagwan' is, he would say:

"What you see here is not 'Dada Bhagwan.' What you see is 'A.M.Patel.' I am a Gnani Purush and He that is manifest within me, is 'Dada Bhagwan'. He is the Lord within. He is within you and everyone else. He has not yet manifest within you, whereas within me he is fully manifest. I myself am not a Bhagwan. I too bow down to Dada Bhagwan within me."

Current link for attaining the knowledge of

Self-Realization (Atmagnan)

"I am personally going to impart siddhis (special spiritual powers) to a few people. After I leave, will there not be a need for them? People of future generations will need this path, won't they?"
~ **Dadashri**

Param Pujya Dadashri used to go from town to town and country-to-country to give satsang and impart the knowledge of

8

the Self as well as knowledge of harmonious worldly interaction to all who came to see him. In his final days in late 1987, he graced Dr. Niruben Amin with the siddhis to continue his Work.

After Param Pujya Dadashri left his mortal body on January 2, 1988, Dr. Niruben continued his Work, traveling within India to cities and villages; and going abroad visiting all continents of the world. She was Dadashri's representative of Akram Vignan, until March 19, 2006, when she left her mortal body entrusting all further care of the Work to Shri Deepakbhai Desai. She was instrumental in expanding the key role of Akram Vignan as the simple and direct path to Self-realization for modern times. Hundreds of thousands of spiritual seekers had taken advantage of this opportunity and are established in the experience of pure Soul while carrying out their worldly duties. They experience freedom, here and now while living their daily life.

Shri Deepakbhai Desai had been given the siddhi to conduct satsang of Akram Vignan by Gnani Purush Dadashri in presence of Pujya Niruben Amin. Between 1988 and 2006, he has given satsang nationally and internationally as directed by Dadashri under the guidance of Dr. Niruben Amin. Now these satsangs and Gnan Vidhis of Akram Vignan continue in full force through the medium of Atmagnani Shri Deepakbhai Desai.

Powerful words in scriptures help the seeker in increasing their desire for liberation and thus they represent the path. The knowledge of the Self is the final goal of all seekers. Without the knowledge of the Self there is no liberation. This knowledge does not exist in books. It exists in the heart of a Gnani. Hence, the knowledge of the Self can only be acquired by meeting a Gnani. Through the scientific approach of the Akram Vignan, even today one can attain Atmagnan, by meeting a living Atmagnani. Only a lit candle can light another candle!

❖ ❖ ❖ ❖ ❖

Preface

Everyone lives their life, but a real life is only that which is free of conflicts.

In the current time cycle of Kaliyug bickering and clashing starts at the time of breakfast, so what remains to be said about the rest of the day? Even in the past time cycles of Satyug, Dwapar and Tretayug, conflicts were present in the homes of prominent people. Even people of purity, such as the *Pandavas,* spent their entire lives planning a battle with the Kavravas. Shri Ramchandraji who was exiled in the forest, had nothing but conflict and friction from the time Sita was abducted, to the point of the Ashvamegh Yagna. Nevertheless, they all overcame conflicts in their lives with spiritual knowledge, and that verily was their special power.

The prime source of all conflicts in life is misunderstanding. "You are the root cause of all your miseries." This statement by Dadashri divulges the very root cause of all miseries with such profoundness, that no one could ever imagine.

If a person continues to paddle his boat of life without deciding on his destination, how will he ever embark upon the right course? He will become fatigued from paddling, give up, and ultimately drown halfway, in the ocean. Therefore, it is very necessary to first, decide the destination. Life without a goal is synonymous to letting an engine run idle. If you want the ultimate goal, then liberation should be that goal. However, if you want something in between, but you do not have happiness in your life, then at least make your life free of conflicts.

Every morning you should pray sincerely and repeat five times, "I do not want to hurt any living being in the slightest extent, with this mind, speech, or body," Despite doing this, if you happen to hurt anyone, then you should sincerely repent and take a vow that you will not hurt anyone again. By doing this, you will wash away your bad deeds and your life will become peaceful.

The bickering and quarrelling between parents and children can only be resolved through understanding. It is primarily the parents who must understand. Excessive attachment will result in a lot of friction and suffering, creating more problems for both the parties involved. You have to fulfill all of your worldly obligations, but by no means are you to perpetuate the cycle of attachment. Dadashri has shed light over parent-children interactions and given us tremendous understanding and insight into this topic. This in turn has improved tremendously the quality of the family life .

Despite the love that exists between husbands and wives, inner conflicts and overt quarrels occur between the two. They are so trapped by their need for security in each other that despite their internal conflicts and quarrels that they continue to live as husband and wife. Through a very informal and jovial approach, Dadashri gives us ways by which husband and wife can attain ideal interactions with each other.

Dadashri also gives us the keys to prevent conflicts between mother-in-law and daughter-in-law, master and servant, a business owner and his customers, and between business partners.

Many aspirants who seek true knowledge do not attain it because they give importance only to the soul, and disregard their worldly life. This one-sided approach renders their knowledge infertile. Real *Gnanis*, like Dadashri have traversed

11

the spiritual realms by maintaining a parallel between both the worldly and spiritual lives. He has given thousands of seekers the ultimate understanding of matters regarding both the worldly and the spiritual life, and within them, instilled tremendous awareness of the two.

In this short compilation, we have put together examples, which have come through the power of Dadashri's speech, whereby we can live an ideal life. Those seeking a more detailed and in depth solution for the worldly life should refer to the long version of Dadashri's books. Books such as, 'Generation Gap,' 'Harmony in Marriage,' 'Speech in Worldly Interactions,' 'Money in Worldly Interactions,' etc., are books which undoubtedly will bring peace to one's life.

- Dr. Niruben Amin

Contents

[1] The Art of Living

[2] Complete Benevolence

[3] Does Suffering Really Exist?

[4] Family Organization

14

15

[6] Business with Principles

[7] Interaction With Subordinates And Employees

[8] Nature's Guest

[9] Human Values

[10] Ideal Interactions

Life Without Conflict

[1] The Art of Living

Life Without a Goal

What is the goal of this life? Do you understand it? Surely, there has to be some goal for this life. A person is born, grows old and is later is carted away to the funeral pyre. The name that was given to him at the time of birth is taken away at that time. The{ are quick to give you a name the moment you are born, to facilitate the worldly interactions and dealings. This is just like naming characters in a play, buv once the play is over, the name is no more. Just as tje name 'Brahtruhari' is given to the king in the drama, the name no longer exists once the play is over. Similarly, you are given a name to carry out your daily living and under this name you acquire your wealth, your hooe, your cars, and money etc. but upon your death it is all taken away. People go through life and then thgy die. Therefore, these two words, 'life' and 'death' mean that every event is a passing circumstance. What is the goal of life? Is it for personal enjoyment, or to serve humankind? Is life for marriage and taking care of your family? Marriage is mandatory and preordained. A person cannot get married if he is not destined to. However, do people not get married even if they do not want to? This is because marriage is preordained for them. Is making a name for yourself the ultimate goal of life? Women such as Sita, Lord Ramas's wife, have made their mark in this world. Their fame stayed here but what did they take with them to their next life? They took their mistakes and entanglements (causes; karmas).

Whether you want liberation (*moksha*) or not, at least come here and obtain clarification of all your entanglements. You will find all the solutions here. Lawyers will charge you a fee to solve your worldly problems, whereas the solution you get here is priceless. You cannot put a price on this solution. Life is full of entanglements. You are not the only one with entanglements; the whole world has them. The world is a puzzle itself.

Religion comes after true understanding. First you have to learn the art of living. One has to become certified in parenting, before getting married. Life is like an engine but it is pointless to keep putting gas in the engine and running it without getting any useful work out of it. There has to be a goal in life. An engine will continue to run in vain but you have to get some work out of it. Unfortunately people live their entire lives, with nothing to show for it, without an achievement. Rather than accomplishments, they create entanglements, which carry forward to their next life.

People's lives have broken down; they have no clue as to what they are living for. They have no awareness about the reason for a birth in the human form. They are not aware that there is a purpose of a human life. What is the goal of the human life? The birth as a human being gives one the ability to choose any future life form, or the choice to attain liberation from further births. No one is aware of the essence of human birth and that is why one continues to wander life after life.

Who Will Teach Us The Art of Living?

Today people are unaware of what is beneficial and harmful in life. The ones, who do have such awareness, have made adjustments according to their intellect (*buddhi*). Their awareness is worldly in nature because it is for attaining only worldly happiness. In reality, even that is not correct. Correctness comes only when one learns the art of living. One becomes a doctor or a lawyer and yet he does not learn anything about the art of living. He learns and masters all kinds of arts except for the art of living.

This art is learnt by approaching the one who is living his life well. Ask such a person to teach you the art of living. Ask him how you should conduct your life; only then will you learn that art. You need to seek out someone who has mastered this art. Unfortunately, no one seems to understand the need to do so. They have totally discarded the importance of the art of living, haven't they? Those living around me will learn this art. However, I cannot say that absolutely no one in this world knows this art.

If a person learns the art of living completely, his life will be easy but he will definitely need religion along with it. Religion is the base for the art of living and it is a necessity. By religion, here I am referring to the code of conduct as prescribed by God. One need not pursue the path of liberation. You must understand the prescribed commands of whomever you have faith in, be it Lord Mahavir, Lord Krishna or any other God. If you cannot practice all of their directives, then at least practice some. Now if celibacy is one of their directives and you get married, then that would be contradicting their directives. In reality there is no contradiction; all they are saying is that you should adjust to the commandments to the best of your ability. Just because you are not able practice two of their commandments, does that mean you discard them all? What do you think? If you are able to abide by only two of their commandments, it is still more than enough.

It is equally important for people to receive a high level

of relative religion (*vyavahaar dharma*). This is the code of conduct for life's daily interactions. This is the art of living. You cannot learn this art through penance, fasting or renunciation of the worldly life. Fast if you develop problems with indigestion.

He who masters the art of living acquires the whole *vyavahar dharma*, but the real religion, the knowledge of the Self (*Atma dharma, nischaya dharma*) will be attained by the one who comes into this world with prior spiritual development. In the *Akram* path (the short-cut, step-less path to Self-realization), one attains the Self through the grace of the *Gnani Purush*. The *Gnani Purush* has the capacity to grace one with both infinite knowledge and infinite worldly wisdom; both are so wonderful that they abolish all kinds of miseries.

Understanding That Leads to Suffering in Life

This *Gnan* is such that it repairs and corrects, and people are such that they ruin and make wrong of everything that is right. They do so because they have the wrong understanding; otherwise there is no suffering in India whatsoever. All suffering is due to lack of right understanding. People blame the government or God for their suffering. Alas people have only learnt to disgrace and defame others.

If a person accidentally ingests poison, will the poison spare him?

Questioner : No it would not.

Dadashri : Why not? He drank it accidentally. Since he did not drink it on purpose, will the poison not let him escape?

Questioner : No, he cannot escape the effect of the poison.

Dadashri : So who kills him? It is the poison that kills him, not God. God does not give suffering or anything else, whatever is done, is done through the body complex (*pudgal*). It is the body complex that gives pain and unhappiness. Is poison also not a body complex? Do we not experience its effect? People of the current time cycle are really the product of their negative tendencies from their past lives. People of the era of previous time cycle used to make do without food and clothes, but people of today, despite having everything, create nothing but conflict. If a man has outstanding taxes, he fears the tax officer and in turn his wife fears him because due to the stress, he mistreats her.

A person, who has all the four necessities of life and yet creates conflict, is nothing but a fool. Does he or does he not get food on time? It does not matter whether the food is cooked in oil or not, but at least he gets his food on time, does he not? Does he also not get his cup of tea on time; whether it is once or twice a day, does he not at least get tea or something to drink? Does he not have clothes to wear? Does he not have a roof over his head? He should be thankful for all this, especially on cold winters days! Therefore, when people complain, in spite of having these basic four necessities, they should be locked up in prison! In spite of having all the four necessities, if a person is still unhappy, then he should get married. You cannot persecute anyone for wanting to get married. Along with these four necessities, marriage is also a necessary component. You cannot say no to anyone who is of age and wants to get married. But so many of those who get married, break their marriages, they wander alone, and invite suffering. What kind of people are these, who get married then break up their marriages? When a person does not have the four or five basic necessities for living, it is understood that he is suffering. Everything else is not really sufferings, but rather difficulties or inconveniences. People however spend their entire day being miserable; all day long they imagine and create mental projections of their so-called sufferings.

In reality it is not the material things that are needed; people's miseries stem purely from ignorance of the Self. Once I give you the knowledge of the Self, all miseries disappear. After that all you have to do is to know where you have not been able to remain within the five *Agnas* that I have given you. That is all you have to do. Even your daily meals are destined and will come at the precise time; that is the force of scientific circumstantial evidences (*vyavasthit*). When the hair on your face grows even against your wish, will the food not arrive without your wish? Your beard will grow even though you do not want it to. What more do you need besides your basic necessities? The more possessions you have, the more difficulties you experience. Before becoming Self-realized were you not getting lost in thoughtful fantasies? Do you recognize fantasies?

Questioner : Yes, I used to have many fantasies.

Dadashri : These thoughts and imaginations are like waves that continue to flow. God has referred to these fantasies as building castles in the air. They are imaginary. People are so caught up in these fantasies. If a person wants to slap someone, he will not do it directly. It would be much better if he did, but instead he makes the subtle inner cardinal mistake of saying, "I will slap him one," and binds karma for another life. The haunting of the 'ghosts of imagination' traps everyone in the world. They haunt people in worrying: 'this is going to happen and if that happens, then this will happen' and on and on.

Materialism and Suffering

The entire world has sunk in the ocean of accumulation and hoarding of unnecessary materialistic things. God has no objection to your accumulation of things that are necessary for life. One should decide on his necessities in life. What are the basic necessities for this body? First and foremost, is air which is available every second, free of cost. Then one needs water and food. The fire of hunger can be doused with simple food, but nowadays people want gourmet food. Clothing and shelter fall under secondary requirements. Is getting respect from others a necessity for living? People go around searching for respect, and become completely veiled in the illusion of life. Should you not learn all this from the *Gnani Purush*?

People would eventually become fed up if sweet water continued to come out of their taps, even if it was only for a day. If you ask them why, they will tell you they prefer plain water. True value of something is not realized until it is no longer available. People go around looking for Coca-Cola and Fanta. Why do you not figure out what your necessities are? Would this body of yours complain if it got fresh air to breath, pure water to drink and some simple food to eat at night? It would not. Therefore decide on the basic necessities for the body. People instead look for a specific flavor of ice cream. Kabir Sahib said:

"No one is your enemy; your enemy is your unnecessary materialism...

Rid yourself of all your needs for unnecessary things, and then you are free to roam about."

Running after unnecessary things in itself is your real enemy.

What are the necessities of this body? If you ask for water for a bath, it is a necessity. The body requires pure ghee and milk, but instead you stuff it with garbage. What good is all the junk food? What do people use to wash their hair? They use shampoo; it looks just like water and soap. These 'sacks of intellect' (Dada referring to people) have discovered things that are not necessary and because of that one's inner happiness has diminished. The Lord had said it is acceptable if there is a difference of five to ten percent between their inner happiness and external happiness, but here we have a difference of ninety percent and that will not do. This big a difference is unnecessary and will eventually kill you, but you will have to suffer in the process. Today so many necessities have been created.

People get worried if the shops were to close for an hour. If you ask them what they need and why they worry, they will say they want some ice cream and cigarettes. Is this not increasing one's dependency on unnecessary things? It is because people do not have internal happiness that, they go searching for it in material things. Whatever internal happiness there once was, is now gone. Do not destroy your inner happiness. People have squandered away this inner happiness, so how can it express? Which is better, to live a natural life or a pretentious one? Youngsters imitate each other. Why should we imitate others? We should be ourselves; people from other countries should imitate us. But a few hippies came to our country and we now imitate them. How can you call this living?

People complain when there is a shortage of refined sugar and brown sugar. Why must you complain about food? As long as you have a stomach, you will manage to find food to eat. You will find enough food to satisfy each tooth. What kind of teeth do you have? There are teeth for tearing, cutting and chewing; nature provides you with everything. And how wonderful are your eyes? Could you find such eyes even if you paid millions of dollars? No, you could not. Some people complain even when they have a million dollars. They do not realize the worth of all the precious things that nature has given them. A person can be content if he simply learned to value just his eyes.

Your own teeth will let you down some day. You give this body food and drink and yet it dies. Death is nature's act of confiscation and repossession. When you die, you will leave everything behind except the entanglements (karmic causes) you created with family, clients, and business associates. God has cautioned, "You mortals! Understand the reality. The possibility of another human birth is extremely rare."

The art of living cannot be found in the current era of this time cycle. Leave aside the path to liberation. Should one not at least know how to live life?

One Must Understand the Beneficial Path

I have a constant awareness of worldly interactions. No watch or radio company has made money off me. I have never purchased such items. What is the use of such things? They are meaningless. Of what use is a watch that causes problems and internal unrest every time it is looked at? There are some children who become very uncomfortable the moment they see their father. If they are playing when they are supposed to be studying, they get nervous when their father walks in; that is how it is with a watch. It unsettles you whenever you look at it, so why not get rid of it? T.V. and radio are direct and present madness.

Questioner : There is a radio in every home.

Dadashri : That is different. What happens where there is no awareness of the Self (*Gnan*)? Attachment (*moha*) prevails. It is attachment when you acquire what is not necessary and economize on what is.

It's like this. It is like bringing home an onion dipped in sugar syrup. You must first decide whether you want to eat the onion or the sugar icing. The onion should be eaten plain otherwise there is no point in eating it. This is all madness. People lack awareness and direction in their decision-making.

If a person sees another person eating an onion dipped in sugar syrup, he will do the same. Onions are such that they become useless when dipped in sugar. People have no awareness; nothing but absolute ignorance prevails within them. They go around with a belief of "I am something." Who are we to tell them otherwise? Even a simple shepherd has this same belief because he owns two cows and two bulls. He believes that he is their superior. He can treat the animals however he wants to. Even if man does not have anyone to control, he ends up being the boss of his wife. How can you deal with someone who has no discretion or awareness of what is appropriate and what is not? Liberation aside, one should at least have some awareness as to what is beneficial and what is harmful in daily living.

You are better off using a cotton bed sheet, which you have paid for rather than using a silk bed sheet, that has been given to you for free. You may question the benefit in doing such a thing. The reason behind this is, if you use things for which you do no have to pay, you become accustomed to it and then when things no longer come free, you have difficulties. Old habits die hard! Everyone in this world is using things without awareness. If we ask prominent religious heads to sleep on a luxurious mattress, they will find it very uncomfortable and will not be able to sleep at night. Some people become accustomed to sleeping on a mat and others on a mattress. God does not accept either the penance of an ascetic or the luxuries of a householder person. God says that only when things are done with an inner awareness, is it correct. If there is no awareness, and you develop a habit, then it is meaningless.

First you must understand what is involved in each path and then you must decide which one you want to follow. If you do not understand, ask 'Dada', he will tell you which paths are hazardous, and which one is the right one. You can then follow that path with his blessings.

You Will Experience Happiness through Such Adjustments

One man came to me asking for my blessing because he did not understand things. I placed my hand on his head and said, "Go. From today onwards, open up a shop of happiness. Get rid of the old shop." What is a shop of happiness? It is a place from where you can give happiness to others, the moment you wake up in the morning. There should be no other kinds of dealings. He understood this very well and started to practice this immediately, and became a happy man. When you start a shop of happiness, happiness will come to you and to those to whom you give. Would you have a need to buy sweets from someone else's shop when you own one yourself? You will be able to eat them whenever you please. Similarly, if you open up your own shop of happiness, you will not have any problems.

You can start any business you want. If you cannot do it every day, do it at least once a week, on Sundays. You will find customers for happiness. The law of *vyavasthit* is such that it will bring customers for you. *Vyavasthit* will bring you customers according to what you have decided.

People open a business of what interests them. Those who like sweets will open a sweet shop. What do people like? Happiness! So why not open a shop of happiness so that you can give happiness to others and at the same time have happiness at home? Eat, drink and enjoy yourself.

Do not invite miseries by thinking about the future. If a person receives a letter saying Chandubhai is going to visit him, he will start to have all kinds of thoughts, even if Chandubhai has not yet arrived.

This Dada is a *Gnani Purush*. How does his 'shop' run so successfully throughout the day? Because his shop is a shop of happiness, he showers happiness even upon those who throw stones at him. The person who throws stones does not realize what he is throwing stones at is a shop of happiness and that he should not do so. He just aims blindly and throws them.

Even when you decide that you do not want to give unhappiness to anyone, will others not give you unhappiness? What will you do then? I will show you a way to handle such situations. One day a week, close your 'post office' and do not accept any 'mail' from anyone and do not send any 'money orders' to anyone either. If someone happens to send you one, keep it aside and say, "The post office is closed today. I will deal with it tomorrow." My post office is always closed!

Why do people behave well on Diwali day? It is because they have a change in their belief for that day. They make a decision that they want to spend the day being happy and so their belief changes and that is why they are able to spend the day being happy. You are the boss and therefore, you have the power to make a similar arrangement too. If you decide that you do not want to be rude to anyone, then you will not be able to be rude that day. You should practice and maintain that rule once a week. Close the post office for one day and relax. Let people complain about it being closed for the day.

Vengeance Is Eliminated, Happiness Increases

Only the intent not to hurt anyone in this world is considered true earning in this life. You should affirm such an intention every morning. Accept any abuse anyone gives you and do not try to analyze what you may have done to merit the abuse. If you accept it, then your karmic account will be cleared on the spot. If you do not accept it and instead retaliate, then that account will continue into your next life and that is what we call 'roonanubandha'. Instead of settling the matter, people retaliate with four times the force. God tells you to give to others what you like to receive yourself. Do not do to others what you would not like done to you. If someone tells you, "You are a good man," you should tell him, "Sir, you too are a good man." If you speak in this manner, it is acceptable.

This entire worldly life is meant for settling past karmic accounts. Any situation that will create vengeance will have to be settled through your becoming a mother-in-law, a wife, a son, or even an ox. You may pay twelve hundred dollars for an ox and it may die the very, next day. Endless life cycles have passed in revenge. Vengeance is the reason you wander life after life in this world. That is why your liberation is impeded. Hindus create enmity in their own homes whereas Muslims quarrel outside of their home; they never create enmity at home. They know they cannot afford to fight with those with whom they have to share the same room with at night. The art of living is to not create enmity with anyone and to become free. That is the very reason some renounce worldly life and run away from their worldly problems. However, one cannot run away from their responsibilities in this manner. From the day of birth, one's life becomes a battle, which needs to be faced. Rather than overcoming life's battles, people fall prey to the luxuries and comforts of the world.

Maintain equanimity when interacting with those around you, whether it is inside or outside your home, the office, or in the public. At home, when you are served food you do not like, accept it gracefully. Do not aggravate anyone. Eat whatever food is served to you on your plate. What is in front of you is an event and if you push it away, you will be the one who will have to pay for it. Therefore, when I am served food I do not like, I take at least two bites. If you do not, you will start a conflict with food itself and with the person who prepared and brought it to you. The food will question, "What wrong have I done? I have come to you. Why are you are insulting me? Eat what you can but do not insult me." Should you not honor the food? Someone may bring a food item that I do not like, but I honor it. Ordinarily it will not come to you but when it does, you have to respect it. This food is your own (earned in your past life) and so when you find faults with whatever is served on your plate, will that increase or decrease your happiness?

Questioner : It decreases.

Dadashri : Why deal with things in a manner that decreases your happiness? You should not conduct yourself or deal with situations in a manner that will cause your happiness to decrease. I am often served vegetables I do not like, but I eat them and I say that the vegetables were very good.

Questioner : Is that not being deceitful? When you say you like something when you actually do not, is that not pacifying the mind unnecessarily?

Dadashri : It is not unnecessarily pacifying the mind. The food will go down your throat easier if you say you like it. When you say you do not like it, you will upset the vegetables, as well as the one who cooked them and your children too, will pick up on your behavior; even your children will assess your worthiness.

Even in my own home no one knows of my likes and dislikes. Is cooking really under the control of the one cooking? The food that ends up on the plate is in accordance with the laws of *vyavasthit* of the one who is going to eat. Therefore, one should not meddle with it.

So Much Luxury and Yet No Enjoyment

Eating in hotels and restaurants can lead to dysentery. When you eat in hotels and restaurants, its effects gradually accumulate inside your body and when the time comes, it will lead to dysentery. The results of any stomach pain will manifest much later. Having experienced this personally, I used to tell everyone not to eat in hotels. I had once gone to a sweet shop and was watching the cook. I saw all kinds of dirt and sweat from the cook fall in the sweet he was making. Nowadays even the food made at home is not hygienic, is it? Hands are not washed when one is binding the dough; there is dirt under the nails. Nowadays they do not cut the nails, do they? Many women have long nails. I ask them if they benefit in keeping their nails long. I tell them to keep their nails long, if there is some benefit, like doing artwork. Then they realize that there is nothing to be gained from it, and agree to cut them. People do not have any sense. They grow their nails and walk around with headphones on their ears. They do not know where their happiness lies. Do they even know about their own Self? All they know is what the world has taught them.

How much prosperity and splendor there is out there to enjoy! You get to travel in the double-decker buses worth hundred thousand rupees for only half a rupee! What comfortable seats! You do not have such seats even in your home. People have so much merit karma (*punya*) but they do not know how to enjoy their rewards, otherwise how can a person in India enjoy riding in a bus that costs a hundred thousand rupees? When you travel by car, do you get covered with dust? No, because we no longer have dirt roads. Your feet do not get dirty. In the past, we had dirt roads and even the kings would come home with dirty feet. People of today, have more luxuries than the kings of the past, yet they do not know how to enjoy the luxuries, do they? Physically, they may be sitting in a bus but internally they are restless.

Worldly Life Runs Naturally and Easily

Truthfully, there is no such thing as suffering, and

whatever suffering there is, is the result of misunderstanding. How many living beings are there in this world? There are infinite living beings but none complain, "We do not have enough," whereas the foolish human beings complain constantly. Has any creature living in the ocean died of hunger? Have you seen any crows die from hunger? No, they only die when they accidentally bump into things or when their life span comes to an end. Have you ever seen a crow shriveled up from hunger? Do dogs ever have to take sleeping pills? How peacefully they fall asleep! It is only the foolish human beings that have to take twenty pills to fall asleep. Sleep is a natural gift; there is real happiness in sleep. Doctors prescribe pills to sedate people. Being sedated is like becoming intoxicated with alcohol. Have you ever seen a crow with high blood pressure? It is only the wretched human beings who are miserable and they are the only ones who need colleges to learn things.

Who teaches the birds to build beautiful nests? Learning to live life comes automatically. Yes, effort (*purusharth*) is required for Self-realization, but you do not have to do anything to carryout your daily living. Only humans are over-wise. Do birds and animals not have women and children? Do they have to get them married? Only humans feel the need to have a wife and children; only the humans are preoccupied with accumulating wealth and getting their children married. You pitiful ones! Why don't you work towards Self-realization instead? There is nothing else worth working for. Whatever you have done so far is worth nothing but crying over in sorrow. Who teaches the young children to steal? It is all in a seed (brought with them from their past life). Why is every leaf of a Neem tree so bitter? It is because the bitterness lies in the seed of the Neem tree. Only human beings are so unhappy, but they are not to be blamed. It was only up until the fourth era of the current time cycle, that there was any happiness. We are now in the fifth era of the time cycle, in which equanimity is unattainable even when one undergoes tremendous penance. Therefore, it is a mistake to look for happiness and harmony in this era of the time cycle.

[2] Complete Benevolence

Two Most Important Activities in Life

What is the purpose of the human life? It is to free yourself completely from the bondage of rebirths. It is to become Absolute, the pure Self, but if you have not acquired the knowledge of the pure Self, then live your life for others. It is only for these two tasks that one gets a birth in India. Does anyone follow these two goals? Instead, people have discovered an art of going from a human form into the animal form by resorting to corruption and deviousness!

Benevolence Creates Merit Karma

Until you achieve liberation, only your merit karma (*punya*) works as your friend and your demerit karma (*paap*) as your enemy. Now you have to decide whether you want a friend or a foe and then ask me how you can encounter a circumstance of a friend or a foe. If someone likes the foe of demerit karma, then I will tell him that he can do whatever he pleases, he can live at the expense of others and go wherever he wants and that he can worry about the consequences later. If however he wants a friend in merit karma, then I will tell him to learn from the trees. Do the trees enjoy their own fruits? Does a rosebush enjoy its own flowers? Not even a little? Maybe when we are not looking? Do they eat their own fruits?

Questioner : No.

Dadashri : These trees are here to serve humans and provide them with fruits. Now how do the trees benefit from that? They progress into a higher life form. The human beings will also progress higher through their help. For example, if you eat a mango, what does the mango tree lose and what do you gain from it? You get pleasure from eating a mango, and because of your happiness there is an improvement in your tendencies and as a result you acquire say, a spiritual earning equivalent to a hundred merit points. From these one hundred points, five percent will go to the mango tree for the fruit it gave you and the remaining ninety-five will remain with you for your progress. Therefore, when you share with others, they come to a higher level and at the same time, you do not fall. You too will progress to a higher level. The trees are really telling you to enjoy all that is theirs.

So if you like this worldly life, if you desire worldly things and can afford to live in this world, practice benevolence through yoga and *upyoga*. Yoga is that done through the mind, body and speech. *'Upyoga'* means to use the intellect, mind and *chit* for the benefit of others. If you do not use them for others, then use them for those at home. Why does a female dog get food to eat? She gets it because she takes care of her puppies, in whom, God resides. The world functions on this very basis. Where do the trees get their nourishment? Do the trees have to make an effort? They never become emotional. Do they ever become emotional? They never feel like going a mile to the river for a drink of water!

Obliging Others Is Helping Yourself

Questioner : What kinds of actions or deeds, are considered good in this world? Can they be defined?

Dadashri : Yes. The actions of the trees are absolutely good actions but the trees do not have a sense of doer-ship. They have life in them; they give their fruits to others. You should do the same. You will keep receiving your fruits: fruits for your mind, your body and your speech. You will keep receiving things as long as you keep giving to others free of charge. You will not experience any difficulties in acquiring any of life's necessities, but if you enjoy the fruits of your good fortune yourself, then you will face difficulties. What will the owner of the mango tree do if the tree were to eat its own fruit? Would he not chop it down? Similarly, people eat their own fruits. Not only that, they also charge a fee for it. They will charge twenty-two rupees to simply fill out a petition. Look what has become of the country where legal advice was free. In fact, it was given over a free meal. If there were a dispute in a village, the wealthy, head businessperson of the village would act as the arbitrator. He would bring the two parties together and make them come to some kind of a settlement. If there were a debt to be satisfied, he would arrange for part of the money to be paid off in cash, and for the balance to be paid off in installments. Then all three would sit down and have a meal together and then go their separate ways. Now, can such lawyers be found today? Therefore, understand the times and act accordingly. If you use your life only for your own benefit, there will be suffering at the time of death. You will not be able to leave this world and your belongings, with equanimity.

If you spend your life for the benefit of others, you will not experience any difficulties, and all of your wishes will be fulfilled. However, if you go around chasing things, none of your wishes will be fulfilled; this approach in life will not let you sleep peacefully. Businessmen today are not able to sleep for days at a time because they have done nothing but cheat and rob people.

Questioner : People want to help others give guidance, but others do not accept their advice or listen to them. What can we do about that?

Dadashri : If a benevolent person looks for the

understanding of the beneficiary, then he is making a judgment on the beneficiary. So do not look for understanding from those you seek to help. A mango tree gives its fruits to everyone but how many mangos does it eat itself?

Questioner : None at all.

Dadashri : Then who are the mangoes for?

Questioner : They are for others.

Dadashri : Yes, does the tree look at whether the person eating its fruit is a good man or a crook? The mango is there for whoever takes it. True benevolent living is the life lived by the trees.

Questioner : But people accuse the very people who help them. Do we still have to continue helping them?

Dadashri : Yes, that is the very thing worth noting. Benevolence towards ingratitude is true benevolence, but where can people acquire such an understanding? If a person understands this much, he is truly blessed. Benevolence is a very high state and it is the ultimate purpose of the human life, and in India, the second aim of a human life is to achieve liberation from the cycle of birth and death.

Questioner : Does ego coexist with benevolence?

Dadashri : The ego of the person who practices benevolence is always within the norm; that ego is always appropriate. The ego of a person who charges a fee for helping others will become very inflated; his ego is so inflated that he really cannot afford to have it inflated anymore.

The law of nature is such that it will take care of those who give their fruits to others. This is the hidden science. This benevolence is relative religion, and then comes real religion, which is the religion of the Soul (*Atma dharma*). The essence of a human life is to use your mind, body and speech for the good of others.

[3] Does Suffering Really Exist?

There Is No Suffering Where There Is the Right Belief

Questioner : Dada, tell us something about suffering. Where does it come from?

Dadashri : If you are the Self, then there is no suffering. If you are 'Chandulal' (the relative self) then there is suffering. If you are the Self, then there is no unhappiness; all suffering will dissolve. "I am Chandulal," is an incorrect belief, "This is my wife, this is my mother, my father, my uncle," are all beliefs; these false beliefs give rise to suffering. If the wrong beliefs go away and the right belief arises, then there is no suffering. People like you whose basic needs are taken care of should experience no suffering. All suffering is the result of wrong beliefs and misunderstanding.

Definition of Suffering

True unhappiness is when you are hungry and you do not get any food to eat for hours on end; it is when you do not get any water to drink when you are thirsty. Would you also not be miserable if you were desperate and were not allowed to go to the toilet? Such miseries can be considered true suffering.

Questioner : That is all fine, but if you look at the world, nine out of ten people are suffering.

Dadashri : Not nine out of ten, but possibly only two out of every thousand are somewhat happy. The rest all continue to suffer from inner turmoil day and night. If you roast sweet potatoes, how many sides will they roast from?

Questioner : How can one take advantage of this constant suffering?

Dadashri : If you analyze the nature of suffering, then it will not feel like suffering. If you do precise and exact *pratikraman* (the process of recalling mistakes, asking for apology and resolving never to repeat it) for your suffering, it will not feel like suffering anymore. People have haphazardly labeled everything as suffering without thinking or analyzing it. For example, you have a set of old sofas and your friend who never had any just bought a new set. When your wife sees them, she comes home and tells you how nice your friend's sofas look and complains that the ones you have at home have become old. Now the suffering has arrived in the home. There was no problem until she saw your friend's sofa, but the moment she set eyes on them, she brought the suffering with her.

If your friend builds a bungalow and you do not have a bungalow, and your wife sees it, she will come home telling you how beautiful your friend's new bungalow is and that you never build anything. That is suffering. These are all self-created sufferings.

If I were a judge, I would first make everyone happy before I sentenced the prisoner. If I had to sentence someone for his crime, I would tell him that it would not be possible for me to sentence him for less than five years. Then if his attorney pleaded for a lesser sentence, I would gradually negotiate the sentence down from four years to three years to two years and finally down to only six months. This way he would go to prison feeling happy that he got away with having to serve only six months. Therefore, suffering is a matter of beliefs. If I were to say six months from the start, he would find it too long.

Maintain Equanimity When Settling Karmic Accounts

You have all the happiness of a king but what can be

done if you do not know how to enjoy it? It's like putting sand in Basmati rice, for which you paid a lot of money. If suffering besieges you, you should say to it, "Why have you come here? I am Dada's *mahatma*. You are not to come here, go somewhere else. You have lost your way." Suffering will go away when you say this. If suffering comes your way, do you have to let it in? You have to tell it to leave. You will not violate your practice of *ahimsa* by doing so! If you insult suffering and unhappiness, it will go away, but you are too kind to them. You do not have to take your practice of non-violence that far!

Questioner : Will suffering not leave through persuasion?

Dadashri : No. You cannot pacify it or persuade it. You have to be stern with it. If you try to pacify it, it will oppose you even more and continue to visit you.

'Varas aho Mahavirana, shurvirata relavajo,
Kayar bano na koi di, kashto sada kampavajo.'
"You are the glorious heirs of Lord Mahavir, let courage flow from you all,
Never allow even a trace of cowardice, and let difficulties tremble in your presence."

Any suffering or difficulty that crosses your path will tremble at the sight of you and will wonder how it managed to get trapped in your home. These difficulties do not own you. You are their master.

How can you be Dada's *mahatma* if difficulties do not tremble in your presence? You can say to the difficulties, "Why did only two of you come? Why did five of you not come? I want to pay you all off." What does our *Gnan* say? It says that the person who insults you does not know 'You' (the Self). You should tell your relative self, "You must have made a mistake. That is why he insulted you. So now remain calm and do not get so excited!" If you do this, your karmic debt will be paid off. Instead, when people have to face difficulties they become so distraught, they say, "I am dead." We all know you only die once but these foolish people will say, "I am dead," so many times over! Can someone who is dead still be living? People do not have to say they are dead all their lives. You just have to know what true suffering is.

Why does this child laugh and not cry when I smack him several times? And why does he cry when you smack him just once? Is it because he feels hurt from the pain? No, he does not cry from the pain, he cries because he feels insulted.

How can you call this suffering? It is suffering when you do not get food to eat or when you do not get to use the toilet. The local authorities have made toilets available in every home. Otherwise, in the old days you had to carry some water in a pot into the forest to relieve yourself. Now you have bathrooms with toilets in your own bedrooms! Even the landlords and the mighty rulers of the past did not enjoy such facilities. They too had to go to the forest. Even they had to run to the forest when they had diarrhea! People unnecessarily go around complaining about trivial things in life. Why are they complaining unnecessarily?

Wrong understanding causes suffering. There is no such thing as suffering if the right understanding is applied. If there is a little infection in your foot, you have to look around to see if anyone else has the same kind of suffering. If you look in a hospital, you will realize what suffering is, while here you suffer unnecessarily with a little infection. You have to investigate all this, don't you? What happens if you suffer without looking at all the facts? How can there be any suffering for people who have so many merit karmas, like yourself? You are born in a family of *punyasadis* (fortunate ones), where you get your meal with very little effort.

Questioner : Each person feels his suffering is greater than others.

Dadashri : That suffering is self-created so you can make it as great as you want to. You can make it forty times greater if you want.

A Worthy Project

Humans do not know how to live life; they have lost the key to living. The key was completely lost but it is a little better now. After the British rule, people have relaxed their rigid ways and do not meddle in other people's affairs. Before, they did nothing but meddle.

People continue to suffer unnecessarily. There is no superior being over you in this world. You are absolutely independent. Even your project or mission in life is independent, but you should go about it in such a manner that you hurt no living being to the slightest degree. Make your project of life as big as this world.

Questioner : Is it possible to do so?

Dadashri : Yes. Mine is very big. I live with the constant awareness that no living being should be hurt by me.

Questioner : But that is not possible for others, is it?

Dadashri : It is not possible, but that does not mean you carry out your project by hurting others. Should there not be some discipline to carry out your mission in a manner that causes the least hurt. I am not asking you to do the impossible.

You Only Have To Have the Inner Intent

Questioner : If there is no such thing as suffering, then how can anyone feel hurt by our actions?

Dadashri : It is because that person does not have the

right understanding. The suffering he experiences is because he believes he is suffering. If you were to slap me, I would not be affected. If you were to slap anyone else, because he believes there is suffering in that, he would suffer. His wrong belief ("I am Chandulal.") remains.

You also have to look at things from the perspective of how you would feel if someone were to slap you. In all situations, keep in mind how you would feel if you were the one on the receiving end.

If you have borrowed ten thousand rupees from someone and your financial circumstances get worse, a thought may cross your mind, "What is the big deal if I do not pay him back?" At that time you should ask yourself, "How would I feel if someone borrowed money from me and did not pay me back?" You must maintain an intellect, which is impartial and just. Your awareness should be, "I would feel very hurt if it were to happen to me, similarly he would feel hurt too and therefore I do want to pay him back." If your intention is such, you will be able to pay him back.

Questioner : The mind will say that this guy is a millionaire and what use is ten thousand for him anyway? He will not be adversely affected it if we do not return it.

Dadashri : You may feel he will not be put in any difficulty but that is not the point. That millionaire counts his rupees when he has to spend it on his son. Have you ever seen money lying around in a millionaire's home? Money is as dear as life to everyone.

Our intention should be that no being in this world should be hurt through our mind, body, or speech.

Questioner : Is that not difficult for an ordinary person to do?

Dadashri : I am not asking you to start behaving that way immediately. All I am telling you is that you need to have a firm inner intent that you do not want to hurt anyone. That inner intent is your firm determination.

[4] Family Organization

What Kind Of Life Is This?

Do you have the knowledge of family organization? In India, we lack the knowledge of how to organize the family. In foreign countries, they do not have the understanding of what it takes to maintain a family. In their culture when children turn twenty, the parents ask them to move out and live on their own, so that the 'love-bird parents' can live by themselves. They say it like it is. If the husband and wife do not get along, they will resort to a divorce. Where are such talks of divorce in our culture? We have to live together all the time. We fight with each other and yet we live together.

This is not the way to live life. It is not considered a family life. If you ask our older ladies how to live life, they will tell you, "Eat and drink in peace, why do you rush through your meals?" First, you must ascertain your necessities and then all the rest is unnecessary. You must also realize it is the unnecessary things that confuses people and makes them take sleeping pills.

Why do conflicts arise in a home? Should you not understand why conflicts arise everyday with your children? Your son talks back to you, you ask a doctor for some guidance. How can he help you when his own wife talks back to him?

We have all kinds of surveys. They have surveys on cotton, on cloves, on this, or that, but no one has done a survey of what is going on within all humans.

Does your fragrance come through at home?

Questioner : What do you mean by 'fragrance'?

Dadashri : Do you keep everyone happy at home? You do not have quarrels at home, do you?

Questioner : They do occur, everyday.

Dadashri : What kind of a person are you? You cannot give peace to your wife or your children? You cannot even make yourself happy? If you want to attain liberation then I will have to reprimand you and if you want to acquire a life in the celestial world, I can show you another simple path, and in that, I will welcome you with respect. I have not forgotten the worldly language. In the days gone by, there used to be differences of opinions between households, but today there are differences of opinions between people within a household. Everyone has a different understanding. There is no awareness of what is beneficial and what is harmful in life.

Untested Father and Untested Mother

People do not even know how to behave as responsible parents. A man excitedly calls out to his wife to come and see what their toddler is doing. "Come quickly and see how smart our boy has become! He stood on his tippy-toes and reached inside my coat pocket and took out some money. Isn't he clever?" The fool! The fool of all fools! Where does a fool like him come from? He has become a father! Is he is not ashamed of himself? Does he even understand what kind of encouragement his son is getting? The toddler watches all this and thinks he has done something great. Now is this something to be proud of? Should there not be some principles? Does it suit us to have our Indian values erode away in this manner? Should parents not have awareness of what kind of talks give the right encouragement to a child? These are all untested (unfit or uncertified) fathers and untested mothers. If a father is a radish and a mother a carrot, then tell me, what will their son turn out to be? Is there a likelihood of him becoming an apple?

Children Respond To Love

A father said something to his son, the son became agitated and so upset that he told his father "You and I will never get along." The father began to plead with his son and told him, "I did not say anything wrong to you son, why are you getting so upset with me?" I asked the father, "Why are you trying to mend fences now? Why did you instigate him in the first place? You should never instigate anyone. These people are very sensitive and quick to react. Do not disturb them. Do not say a thing, just eat, drink and enjoy yourself."

Questioner : Is it not a parent's duty to caution their children if they get on a wrong path?

Dadashri : It's like this, people can caution their children as parents, but do we have any real parents today?

Questioner : Whom do you consider a good parent?

Dadashri : True parents will tell their son he is walking down the wrong path of life, and upon telling him, the son will stop his wrongdoings. That is the definition of true parents. Where can you find such love these days? Today's parents do not have love. The world can only be won through love. The love parents have for their children today is comparable to the love a gardener has for his rosebush. How can you call parents of today, 'parents'? They are uncertified fathers and uncertified mothers! So what kind of a state will their children be in? One should only be allowed to get married after he or she has been tested and become certified as a parent. When even the Government does not give you a job without a test and a certificate, how can you get married without a certificate? The

responsibility of a parent is greater than that of the Prime
Minister of India. It is a higher status than that of a Prime
Minister.

Questioner : What is the definition of a certified father
or mother?

Dadashri : Uncertified fathers and mothers are the ones
whose children do not listen to them or obey their instructions;
their children do not like them and they cause problems for
them. Are parents today not uncertified?

Otherwise Remain Silent and Just Observe

A Sindhi gentleman asked me what he should do to
improve his two sons. I replied, "Why did you bring sons like
them? Could you not have selected them? All mangos are
mangos and they even look alike but still we sample them
before we buy them. If you bought two tasteless mangos, two
sweet ones, two sour ones and two bad ones, how can you
expect to have sweet mango juice? What is the point of fussing
about it later? If you brought home a sour mango, to know it
as sour, is *Gnan*. When you get a sour taste, observe that taste.
You have to observe the *prakruti* (inherent nature). It is not
under anyone's control. Every circumstance or an event is a
natural creation. No one can interfere in it nor can anyone
change it and it is *vyavasthit*.

Questioner : Do children not improve through spanking?

Dadashri : They will never improve. Physical punishment
improves nothing. Try hitting this machine. It will break. The
children too, will break. They may appear intact on the outside,
but they are broken from within. If you do not know how to
give encouragement to others, then remain silent and just drink
your tea quietly. Just watch everyone's faces. Observe the two
mannequins fighting with each other; you simply have to

observe them. You have no control over any of this. You are just the knower.

Those who want to increase their ties to this worldly life may fight and do whatever they please, but to those who want liberation, I tell them to simply see what unfolds.

Nothing improves in this world through reproach. The person who rebukes merely inflates his own ego in thinking, "I really told him off!" But, if you look deeper, his reproach did not have any effect on the person he told off. Brass will remain brass and bronze will remain bronze. If you keep beating brass, will you be able to prevent it from discoloring? No. Why is that? It is because one of the inherent properties of brass is its proneness to discoloration. So, you should just remain quiet. Just because you do not like a particular scene in a movie, do you have the right to go and burn the screen? No, you have to observe that too. Is every scene going to be to your liking? Instead, people get up on their seats and start shouting, "Hey! He will kill you, he will kill you!" As if they are so compassionate! All this is to be observed. Eat drink, watch and enjoy yourselves.

You Only Need To Improve Your Self

Questioner : Children defy their teachers, so when will they improve?

Dadashri : The one who suffers is the one at fault. The fault is of the sufferer. The teachers and the gurus are the dimwitted fools and that is why their students are disrespectful and insolent towards them. The children are good but it is the teachers and parents who are brainless. Adults insist upon their old ways so naturally the young are bound to retaliate. Today parents' conduct is such that their children will be insolent. The conduct of adults has declined and that is why children act the way they do. If there is an ongoing positive change in a person's thoughts, speech and actions he can become the supreme Lord and if the changes are negative, he can become a demon.

People destroy everything by trying to improve others. You have to improve yourself before you can improve others. How can you improve others without improving yourself? Therefore, tend to your own garden first before you look at someone else's. If you look after your own garden, your harvest will be fruitful.

Do Not Meddle but Adjust

Worldly life is that which is ever changing. It is constantly changing but the older generation is stuck in their old ways. You should change with the times, if you do not, you will die suffering. You must adjust according to the times. I adjust with everyone, even with a thief. When I talk to a thief, he will realize my compassion. I do not tell a thief what he is doing is wrong because it is his viewpoint, whereas people in general will call him a liar, a cheater and all kinds of unworthy names. But these lawyers today, are they not cheaters and liars too? They defend and win bogus cases; are they not being deceitful too? You say a thief is deceitful but how can you trust a person who defends fraudulent cases? And how can you trust anyone who defends the actions of the lawyer? Despite this, does the life of a lawyer not go on? I never tell anybody that he or she is wrong. Each is correct from his viewpoint. But you can explain to them what the consequences of stealing will be.

When old people enter a home, they start meddling and ask all kinds of questions: "Why do you need this big a TV? Why do you need a radio?" They should stop such foolish meddling and instead try to make friends with the youngsters. The world will continue to change; nothing remains the same. The youngsters are bound to get attracted to new things and, there is an endless flow of new things. Things come and go but the elderly should not meddle with that. They do not have to do anything that does not suit them. If they do not like ice cream, they do not have to eat it but instead many become contemptuous towards it. These differences of opinions arise because of the changing times. Children behave according to the times. The very definition of illusion (*moha*) is that new things keep coming out and will continue to attract the beholder. From a very young age, I had come to a conclusion through my intellect, that this world was changing constantly, for better or for worse. And, I also concluded that no one has the ability or the power to change this world. Nevertheless, I am saying that you should change and adjust according to the times. If your son wears a new hat, do not say, "Where on earth did you get that?" Instead, just compliment him on the cap and ask him, "Where did you buy such a nice cap? How much was it? Did you get it on sale?" Adjust in this way.

Have you seen youngsters walk around with their headphones (walkman)? It is a newfound interest that has come into these poor children's lives. This is a new phase in their development. If one were spiritually developed, he would lose interest in it and not go around with it stuck on his ears all day. After trying a new thing once, he would lose interest. New fads have to be experienced just once, not continuously. This is a new kind of fascination for their ears and that is why they listen to the headphones all day long.

They have newly begun their life in the human form. Those who have passed through the human life form thousands of times, will not continue to be fascinated by anything.

Questioner : Children like to go out a lot.

Dadashri : Children are not tied or bound to us; everyone is in his or her individual bondage. All you can do is to ask them to come home early, and after that, whatever time they come home, is *vyavasthit*. You have to carry out all your worldly duties, but they should be carried out without any *kashayas* (anger, deceit, pride or greed). All worldly interactions without *kashaya* is *moksha,* and any worldly interaction with *kashaya* is bondage for more worldly life.

Questioner : My nephew wakes up at nine everyday and does not do any work, what should I do?

Dadashri : Simply put a blanket over him and tell him to sleep peacefully because that is his nature. Some people get up late and work hard, while other unfortunate ones wake up as early as four in the morning yet still accomplish nothing. I too, used to be late in everything. I would leave home only after I heard the school bell and then had to listen to my teacher's scolding. How can the teacher know my nature? Everyone's 'Rustons' (a make of an engine) and pistons are different.

Questioner : It is difficult to maintain discipline if one is late, is it not?

Dadashri : Bickering at him is the indiscipline. Stop the bickering and ask Dada a hundred times a day, for the power and strength to do so. Ask and you will receive.

The questioner understood Dada's instructions and he put them in practice. Everyone in the household stopped bickering and nagging the nephew about getting up late. Consequently, within a week, he began to wake up at seven and started working harder than anyone else.

Silence Is a Powerful Weapon

In the current times, there is nothing better than speaking as little as possible. Today the words that come out hurt people like rocks. This goes for everyone, therefore it is better to say as little as possible. It is not worth saying or telling anyone, anything. On the contrary, you make things worse by your words. If you tell someone not to be late for the train, he will end up being late and if you do not say a word, he will be on time. Everything works fine if you remain silent. Your words are nothing but ego. Children will start to improve from the day you stop nagging them. The words you utter are not helpful and that is why they become agitated. Children do not accept your words and that is why your words bounce back. You should carry out your duties of providing food and shelter for your children and fulfill all your obligations; nothing else is worth doing or saying. Do you understand that you will not gain anything by telling them anything? The children are grown up now. Are they likely to fall down the stairs now? Why are you neglecting your own spiritual welfare? Your duty towards children is a relative duty. It is not worth interfering in it. Instead of bickering, it is better if you just remain silent. You ruin your mind and the minds of others by bickering.

Questioner : Children do not understand their responsibilities.

Dadashri : The responsibility lies in the hands of *vyavasthit*. Children are aware of their responsibilities but because you do not know how to communicate with them, you make a mess of things. Your recommendations are only correct if the children follow them. If parents talk nonsense, children's behavior will be senseless too.

Questioner : Children talk back rudely.

Dadashri : Yes, but how will you stop them? If you stop talking back to them, they will too, and all unnecessary hurtful words will cease. Only then will everyone benefit.

If you get into a disagreement with someone, it will create

a like of prejudice causing the other person to have a negative opinion about you. You must simply remain silent and try to have faith in him. Nothing improves by nagging. Improvement comes only through the words of a *Gnani*. Parents have tremendous responsibility towards their children. Can you not get by without telling them anything? Yes you can get by and that is why the Lord has said for us to act as if we are dead as far as all the negativities in the world are concerned. God has said to live as if you are dead to this world. Whatever is ruined, can be improved. You do not have to cut off and abandon what is ruined. You should not try to improve what is ruined. Leave that task to me. I can improve whatever is ruined, but you should not try to do so. You should simply follow my instructions. Only the one who has improved himself can improve others. How can you improve others when you yourself have not yet improved?

Follow this specific instruction of mine if you want to improve your children. Take a vow of silence for six months. Speak only when children ask you something, but you should tell them you would appreciate it if they did not ask you anything. For any negative thoughts that arise towards your children, immediately do *pratikraman*.

Remain Superficial In Relationships

You carry a baby for nine months and when the baby is born, you have to help him or her walk and get around in the world. You should only do this when they are young. After that, you should let go. Do cows not do the same to their young also? You need to guide and correct your child until the age of five, after that you cannot correct him, and after the age of twenty, his wife will improve him. You do not have to do that.

You have to be superficial in your relationship with your

child. In reality, no one belongs to you. Your child is yours only through a physical relation with your body. Will any one of the children come with you when you are being cremated? Those who become attached to their children and think that their children belong to them, will suffer a lot. Your feeling of 'mine' will be of no help to you. Children are yours from the worldly, relative perspective. If the child is hurt, you should give him medical attention and treatment, but do you have to cry in the process?

Is a woman likely to lactate for her stepchild? No, so keep the same relationship with your own children. This current time cycle is that of the *Kaliyug* (age of quarrel and destruction). All relationships are relative. Keep relative as relative. Do not consider them as real. If your relationship with your son were real, then you could tell him to leave your home until he improves. But, these relationships are all relative and therefore you must adjust everywhere. You have not come here in this world to improve anyone. You are here to free yourself from the bondage of karma. Instead of trying to improve others, just maintain a positive, inner intent. Only a *Gnani Purush*, who is faultless, can improve others, so take your children to him. Why do they become spoilt? They become spoilt because of your meddling. Interference and meddling is the cause that ruins everything in the world. Even this dog will bite you if you irritate it. What happens when you irritate human beings? They too will bite. So do not irritate them.

There is infinite scriptural knowledge in every word I speak. If a person understands these words and acts accordingly, he will achieve salvation. This science is such that you will have to take only one more birth before achieving liberation! You will forego hundreds of thousands of rebirths. With this science, you will get rid of all your attachment and abhorrence and become *vitarag* (void of attachment). When you achieve a state of *aguru-lagu* (balanced state of the Self) there will be endless advantage of this science.

Give Advice Only As a Last Resort

If you become free of your intellect (*abuddha*) like me, then your spiritual work will be done. The moment you use your intellect, the world will emerge in front of you. At home, you should speak and answer only when they ask you something, and when they do ask you for your opinion, keep a resolve within that it would be better if they did not ask you anything. If they do not ask you anything, then you would not be required to use your intellect.

All traditional values in the world are gone, there is a tremendous influence of the current time cycle on people and all moral and honorable values have completely disintegrated. No one has the ability to make others understand anything. If a father says something to his son, the son will say, "I do not want any advice from you." Why are your children not ready to listen to what you have to say? It's because what you say is not the truth. Would they not listen if it were the truth? Parents give advice because of their attachment. They ruin their own future births because of their attachment.

Resolve Everything in this Very Life Time

Vyavasthit runs everything in this world. Therefore, there is no need to say anything. The only thing worth pursuing and acquiring is your own religion, the Self. You used to think that you were the doer, but now you must erase that belief. You are no longer the doer, are you? You do not have to run anything, do you? Everyone is a 'top' that spins as dictated by his or her own karma (the winding of karma of past life are dissipating in this life, just as a top dissipates energy as it spins). Let go of all the suffering! Glasses may break, the soup may boil over, the wife may scold the children but all the while, you should just look the other way and sit down comfortably. They can only accuse you of not saying anything if they see you paying attention to everything. If nothing else, just turn the rosary. If they see you doing that, they will not bother you. Besides what have you to do with all of that anyway? Nagging is fine if you are going to live forever, otherwise it is not worth saying anything. Even cows talk to their offspring politely, but they do not talk excessively, whereas humans keep nagging until they die. Those who nag are foolish; they destroy their homes (family). When can there be an end to all this? For endless lives, you have wandered about the worldly life without doing any good for yourself or others. Only he, who has done well for himself by being free from attachment, can do the same for others.

Why Invite Unnecessary Suffering?

If your child is sick, nurse and take care of him the best you can, but do it in a superficial manner. How should you relate to your children? Relate to them as though they are your stepchildren! As a mother, you can say, 'my children' and the children can say 'my mother,' but from within, the bond should not run deep. Therefore, in this current time cycle, keep your relationship with your children like they are your stepchildren, otherwise you will be doomed. Children are not the ones who will take you to *moksha*. Your children will become wise, if you become wise yourself. Is excessive affection a thing to be given to children? These children, for whom you have so much affection, are the very people who will stab you. Affection and attachment will turn into abhorrence. You should live as if you are being forced to love them. On the surface you can say, "I love you," but from within you should know you are showing this love because you have to, and that this relationship is not real. You will realize exactly what this true relationship with your son is all about if you hit and reprimand him for one hour. If he were truly your son, then even after the beating, he would get down on his knees and say to you, "Dad, your hand must be hurting a lot after the beating." If he says that, then your relationship is real. But if you were to rebuke him for just an hour, he would stand up to you and hit you. You are attracted to your children because of your attachment (*moha*). A real son is one who would willingly enter the funeral pyre with his father. Has any son ever done that?

All of your suffering comes because you take it upon yourself. Your children do not ask you to shower your affection on them, but fathers themselves are guilty of doing this. The fault is entirely yours. You have to carry out all your responsibilities and duties as a father. One father was hugging his child so hard that the child bit him. The real Self cannot be anyone's son or a father. In this *Kaliyug*, your children have come to you as your creditors; they have come to collect on a debt from your past. What if you were to tell your customers, "I do not like it without you; I miss you."? What would they do? They would hit you. All these relationships are relative, and from these, evolve all the inner enemies of anger, pride, deceit and greed, attachment, and abhorrence. From the inner enemy of attachment arises the enemy of abhorrence. You should never become drawn into any *kashaya* that arises. If the milk is boiling over, you just have cut down the heat.

Correct Molding and Incorrect Molding

Questioner : In dealing with my children, I do not understand what is proper and what is improper.

Dadashri : Whatever you do without being asked, is being over-wise. However, you should carry out your duties towards your children; until they reach the age of five, you should do everything for them. Later, when they are older, if your son asks you for his school fees, you should tell him, "Son, when you need money you have to tell me a few days in advance. Money doesn't come easily. I have to make arrangements to borrow that money." Then you should give him the money, the next day. You should make them aware of the fact that money does not come easily. Otherwise, they will think money comes easy, as if it is flowing from a tap. You should interact with your children in a manner that helps maintain a stable relationship. At the same time, they must not become spoilt and become your oppressors. Parents tend to show so much affection towards their children that they become spoilt. Should there be excessive affection? Do you have such affection for a goat? What is the difference between a goat and your child? They both have souls within them. There should neither be excessive affection, nor disinterest in them. You can tell them that as long as you are alive, you will always be there for them whenever they run into any difficulties. Do not meddle in their affairs unless they are in some difficulty. Do not get excited if you see your child drop money from his pocket. He will know it when he realizes it himself. Why should you call out unnecessarily? Why should you create unnecessary havoc? Besides what would he do if you were not around? Everything is in the hands of *vyavasthit* but you meddle in everything unnecessarily. Even your bodily functions are in the hands of *vyvasthit* and whatever is yours, the Self, remains with you. The only effort (*purushartha*) you have to make is to remain in the Self and it is that which is considered your true effort. This is where you have your own independent control. Absolutely no effort or control is required as far as this physical body is concerned. The physical body is completely dependent upon your *prakruti* (the inherent nature of your relative-self).

Once the ego awakens in the child, you cannot say anything to him. Why must you say anything? He will learn from his own mistakes. You are at liberty to tell him anything, until he reaches the age of five. Between the ages of five and sixteen, you may even have to spank him a little if the occasion arises. Even after the age of twenty, you cannot say a word to him. To say anything is a crime. He may even kill you one day.

Questioner : Has this puzzle arisen because parents have become uncertified fathers and mothers?

Dadashri : Yes, otherwise children would not be the way they are. They would be very obedient. It is the parents who have no substance. The soil is bad, the seeds are bad, the goods are bad and yet parents claim and believe their children will be like Lord Mahavir! How on earth can they be like Mahavir? What must be the qualities of a mother who is to raise a *mahavir* (great soul)! If the father is not quite up to par, it will do, but what should the mother be like?

Questioner : So should we not even think about trying to mold our child or teach them moral values?

Dadashri : There is nothing wrong in thinking.

Questioner : The schools take care of their academic education, but what about the development of their morals and character?

Dadashri : Leave their molding and development to the jeweler. Those who are expert at it will do the molding. You can say things to your child until he is about fifteen years old; you can mold and shape him to be like you, but later, his wife will take over. People do not have the skills or the knowledge of how to mold others, and yet they keep doing it. That is why their molding is not successful. The nose (his ego) ends up being two inches longer than it should be and later his wife will come and reduce it to size! Then he will try to do the same to her and so starts the conflicts between them.

Remain Dramatic in Everything that is Mandatory

This is a drama! Life is a drama. How can you make the sons and daughters in a play, yours forever? Yes, there is nothing wrong in saying, "This is my son. May he live a hundred years," but you have to say it in a very superficial manner, as if you are acting in a play. For believing all these relations to be real, you have to do *pratikraman*. Wherever you have perceived something to be real when in reality, it is not, attachment and abhorrence arise. However, through *pratikraman*, you will attain liberation. *Alochana, pratikraman,* and *pratyakhyan*, as shown by Dada, leads to liberation (*alochana* = confession; *pratikraman* = repenting; *pratyakhyan* = avowal not to repeat the mistake).

This worldly life is nothing but a big joke. What would your son say if you were to fight with him for an hour? "Either you leave or I will leave," he would say. Then you as a father would retort, "I will not give you your inheritance." The son would then question, "Who are you to stop me from receiving it?" He will be sure to procure his inheritance by any means necessary. There was one son who offered his lawyer an additional three hundred rupees to humiliate his father. The father told his son, "Had I known you were going to turn out like this, I would have killed you the day you were born!" The son responded, "It truly is a miracle that you did not." How could the father have killed his son if his karma had destined him to be insulted in this manner by his son? There have been countless such incidents, which, had you been a witness to, your eardrums would have burst! You pitiful people, let it be known that incidents much worse than this have occurred! So now, turn towards your Self. There is nothing but ghosts in the non-self, no matter where you go.

For a female dog, nursing her puppies is a mandatory act;

it is not an act of benevolence. If a calf did not nurse from its mother, the cow would be miserable from the pain. Mothers feed their youngsters for their own benefit. Fathers raise their children for their own benefit, what is extraordinary about that? It is all mandatory.

Handle Children like Glass

Questioner : Dada, my children misbehave at home. My scolding has no effect on them.

Dadashri : Have you ever noticed the writing on some packages shipped on the trains? Do they not say, 'Glass-Handle With Care,'? Similarly, you should practice the same policy at home when interacting with your children. What happens to glass if you keep hitting it with a hammer? No matter how upset you are, would you throw that package of glass? Would you not regard the label, right away? Likewise, you should handle everyone at home as if you are handling glass. Typically if something goes wrong within the home, your immediate response is, "Why did you lose your purse? Where did you go? How did you manage to lose your purse?" This kind of bombardment is same as hitting glass with a hammer. If parents simply understand the statement, 'Glass- Handle With Care,' they will be able to deal with the children. They need not be Self-realized for this.

Love is the only way to improve the world. What the world calls 'love' is not real love; it is infatuation, attachment. You love your daughter, but would that love exist if she were to do something wrong? At that time, you get upset with her and therefore it is not love, it is infatuation or attachment.

Live with your children as though you are their trustee. Do not worry or harbor anxieties about getting them married. Whatever happens, just say, "It is correct." You will gain nothing by saying, "It is incorrect." Those who perceive it as wrong or incorrect, suffer a lot. Of course if a couple's only child were to die, you cannot tell them, "It is correct." In instances such as that, you must say what happened to their child was very unfortunate. You must express your feelings naturally. You have to play out your role in the drama of life, but from within, your conviction should be that whatever happens is 'correct' and move on. Glass is a glass as long it is in your hands and if it slips and breaks, then say it is correct. Tell your daughter to be careful as she picks up the broken glass, but from within say that it is correct.

If your speech does not have anger in it, it will not hurt the other person. Words spoken in anger are not the only form of anger. Anger also exists as anguish churning within a person. To suffer in silence and to tolerate is twice the anger. Tolerance is similar to putting pressure on a coil. The coil can only sustain so much pressure. Similarly, one can only tolerate so much before his 'spring' recoils. The breaking point of one's tolerance level will be realized when his spring shoots from having an excessive amount of pressure exerted upon it. Why do you have to tolerate? You have to solve everything through *Gnan*. If any damage occurs to you or your relative world, you are to simply remain an observer (*drashta*) and a knower (*gnata*) of everything that is going on. This world is only meant to be seen and to be known.

The Home Is a Garden

One man came to me and began complaining about his wife. I asked him what his wife was complaining about and he told me she went around saying, "My husband is shameless and stupid; he has no sense." Why must people look for their own justice in marital matters? He told me his home was ruined and his wife and children were spoilt. I told him nothing had been ruined, and that he did not know how to perceive things. He simply did not know how to look at the human beings in his own home. I told him that his home was a beautiful garden. In the past time cycles of *Satyug , Dwaparyug* and *Tretayug*, people's homes were like farms. Some were rose farms, others were carnation farms, and others were jasmine farms. In the present time cycle of *Kaliyug*, the farms have been replaced with gardens, in which you will find all kinds of flowers. You as a head of the household are a rose, but you also expect everyone else in your home to be like a rose. You tell others in your home, "You are not like me. You are a carnation. Why is your color white? I want you to bloom and smell like me." This is how you keep beating them down. You foolish people! At least learn to recognize the different flowers. You only have to recognize and understand each *prakruti*. What kind of a flower is this? You should continue to watch each plant until it bears flowers and fruits to see what kind of a plant it is. Just observe the differences and when the buds on the plant bloom into flowers, you will realize what kind of plant it is. Therefore, interact with that plant with this information in mind. You have to behave according to the other person's *prakruti*. In the past, everyone in the family, the wife and the children, behaved according to the commands of the eldest man of the household, whereas today in *Kaliyug*, everyone's *prakruti* is different and incompatible with each other. That is why, in the current times it is necessary for you to adjust with each person's *prakruti* in your home in order to get your work done. If you do not, you will ruin your relationships. Become a gardener and take care of your garden. Your wife's *prakruti* is different; your son and daughter's *prakrutis* are different. Take advantage of each *prakruti*. All relationships are relative, including the one you have with your wife. This body of yours too, is relative. Relative means they will leave you if you if you spoil your relationship with them.

The power to change anyone is nonexistent in this day and age, and therefore, you should not expect any changes to occur. You can improve others only if there is unity between your mind, body and speech. People will improve only if whatever is in the mind is expressed precisely through the speech and conduct. Today, this is not so. Bring normality, act according to what the situation calls for when you deal with everyone at home.

What Is There To Become So Captivated About?

Many grandfathers are thrilled when their grandchildren call them, 'Grandpa'. If they do not call them 'grandpa', are they going to call them 'uncle'? They may call them 'Grandpa,' but they understand from within, that 'Grandpa' is going to die some time soon. Grandpas are mangos that have gone bad and need to be discarded, and yet the grandfather finds it thrilling to be a grandpa. Alas! This is what the world is like. When a child speaks in a baby talk, "Daddy, come daddy, Mommy is calling you for tea," the father becomes titillated from within, just like a happy bull! He feels he is the only father in the world. Who does he thinks he is? Let go of this madness! Even dogs, cats and the donkeys are fathers; tell me who is *not* a father! All conflicts in the world are because of this only.

A man is truly worthy of being glorified if after discovering the reality of life, he decides he does not want to become a father, otherwise many men become daddies, do they not? If the boss reprimands him at work, when he comes home and his child calls out to him, 'Daddy, daddy,' he forgets everything. This is similar to the effect of wine; it intoxicates people and makes them forget everything.

If a couple, who had been childless for a long time, suddenly had a son, the father would be overjoyed. However, if the son were to then die, he would cry just as much as he had

laughed when his son was born. Therefore, fathers need to be
aware of what would become of them if they child were to ever
die. Therefore stop rejoicing from today, so that there will be
no sorrow. In which previous life were you without children? It
is nothing new. Even the cats, the dogs and the animals have
children too!

Worldly Interaction Should Be Within Normal Limits

Maintain normality in everything; maintain love in one eye
and sternness in the other. Sternness does not cause as much
harm to others as anger does. Sternness is just a show of anger
without the hurting of others. I too, had to be stern with my
workers and ask them, "Why are you not working?" Certain
situations require that you deal with them in a certain manner.
You must act according to what the situation calls for.

In worldly interactions, an appropriate response is
required, depending on the situation. If an appropriate response
is lacking, the interaction becomes spoiled.

One bank manager told me, "I remain perfectly calm at
home. I do not say a word to my wife or my children." I told
him he was the ultimate fool and that he was not worth anything
in this world. He thought that Dada would be very happy with
him and reward him. The fool! Can there be a reward for this?
If your child does something wrong, you have to question why
he did it and tell him not to do it again. You have to say it in
a make-believe way, as if you mean it (show emotions without
being emotional), otherwise he will think whatever he is doing
is fine because by not saying anything, you accept his actions.
Children fall apart because you do not say anything to them.
You have to tell them everything, but it has to be in a 'dramatic'
manner. You have to sit him down at night and talk to him,
explain things to him. Children need to be shaken up a little,
now and then. Although they have some good qualities, you

have to shake them a little. Is there anything wrong in doing so?

Questioner : Dada, my son makes fifteen hundred rupees a month and I am retired. I live with him and his wife. They both keep criticizing me the way I do things or ask me why I go out. I am going to tell them that I am going to leave their home.

Dadashri : Do they feed you well?

Questioner : Yes, Dada they do.

Dadashri : Then you cannot tell them you will leave, because having said so you may not be able to leave and you will have to swallow your own words.

Questioner : So then, should I not say anything to them?

Dadashri : If you have to, then tell them very calmly, "It would be good if you did things this way, but really it is up to you." If there is a possibility of changing others through your actions, then go ahead and do it, otherwise you are likely to aggravate them. So in that case, it is best not to say or do anything.

For example, a father has four sons. He constantly rebukes the two who do nothing wrong but says nothing to the other two who are constantly doing something wrong. The father is the way he is because of their own karmic accounts.

Have No Expectations From Children

Questioner : Why do parents use the word *'chiranjivi'* (Long live) to address their children?

Dadashri : If they do not write *'chiranjivi'*, then some other word will creep in. Do parents not have a desire to see their son grow up to be a happy man before they die? Nevertheless, there is also an expectation that he will take care of them when they get old. Why do people grow mango trees? To eat the mangos! But let me tell you what kind of a mango tree the children of today are. They will bear only two mangos of their own and will ask their parents for two more! Therefore, do not have any expectations of them.

A man came to me one day and said that his son had asked him whether he should send him a hundred rupees every month. He said he told his son, "Son I do not need your Basmati rice (luxury food), I get a crop of millet (basic simple food) that sustains me. Now why would I start such new business of this kind? I am satisfied with what I have."

Be a Friend

Questioner : Should we think of our children as our guests?

Dadashri : There is no need to do that. There is one way to improve your children, be a friend to them. I adopted this behavior at a very young age. I have maintained friendships with the young and the old. Nurture a friendship with your children. Children are looking for love but they do not find that love. Then they suffer in silence, they can neither talk to anyone nor can they bear the suffering. I have a solution for the troubled youngsters of today. I have directions as to how to guide them. The love, which has manifested within me, is such that it will neither increase nor decrease. That which increases or decreases is not love, but infatuation. That which does not increase or decrease is pure love. Everyone will surrender to such love. I do not want to control anyone and yet everyone surrenders to this love. I am merely instrumental in the process.

The Dawn of Religion

Questioner : Why is religion declining in this new generation?

Dadashri : Religion has already deteriorated. There is nothing left to deteriorate. Now there is a rise in religion. A new beginning comes only after a decline. Just as there is ebb and tide in the ocean, this world too operates on the principle of ebb and tide. Man cannot survive without religion. Other than religion, what other support does man have?

Children are mirrors; they reflect the mistakes that lie within the parents.

A father cannot sleep at night worrying about his son, but his son sleeps peacefully. Here, the fault lies with the father. I told one such father, "You are the one at fault in this. You had spoilt your child in the past life and that too, for your personal gain." This fact is worth understanding. What can a child do if he is born to an uncertified father and mother? Men become fathers around the age of twenty to twenty-five. Their own fathers complain about them and yet they become fathers without any certification. How can you blame the son? Children will come and tell me about all their wrongdoings, they will even confess to stealing. Confession is to be made only to a great spiritual master. There will be some extraordinary changes in India.

The Aura Of Fire: The Aura Of Respect

Questioner : Dada graces us so that there will be peace in our home and that we may progress in our spirituality.

Dadashri : Yes, not just for peace in your homes but also so that your children will learn high moral value by observing you, such is this *Gnan*. Children have become mad from watching their parents' madness. Parents do not have appropriate thoughts or conduct. Husband and wife behave inappropriately in front of their children, so what do you expect from the children? What kind of impression does that have on them? Surely, you need to maintain boundaries. What kind of an aura does fire have? Even small children respect fire, do they not? The parents need to have such aura of respect.

The minds of parents today have become confused and broken. They speak as they please; their words are hurtful. That is why children have become bad. The husband speaks hurtfully to his wife and vice versa. A puzzle has arisen. This should not be so in India. However, this is one of the effects of the current time cycle of *Kaliyug* and so it will always be this way. In all this, it is indeed a wonder that such a phenomenal Science has arisen. Whoever encounters it, will attain liberation.

Deep Inner Intent Is the Final Key

Questioner : What should we do when our children get on the wrong path?

Dadashri : When they get on the wrong path, you have to remain as an observer and a knower. Keep a prayerful attitude for their welfare. Pray to the Lord to grace them.

You have to understand and accept whatever happens is correct. The fault decidedly is of the sufferer. The Lord has said, "If you improve, then everything else will improve in your presence."

You should explain to your young children that every morning after their bath, they should worship the Sun Lord, and ask and pray for right intellect for themselves and the world and for the salvation of the world. If they do this much, they will be instilled with right values. This way the parents become free from their karmic bondage with them.

Everything in life is mandatory. You have no choice in the matter. Even if you borrow money for your son's education, if he behaves insolently towards you, you cannot remind him of the sacrifices you have made for him, because you are duty-bound and obliged to do so. You did what was mandatory. You should carry out all your duties.

[5] Understanding Brings Radiance To Your Home Life

How to Resolve Differences of Opinions

A very strange time is coming. There will be storm after storm. Therefore, be vigilant. Just as we have hurricanes and storms in the atmosphere, there will be many natural catastrophes. Human beings will have to face tremendous difficulties. As such, people have so many difficulties in life; everyone is roasting like potatoes in a fire from all directions. People do not understand what they are living for. They have also lost faith in themselves. What can be done now? At home, people have conflicts with their family and do not know how to resolve them. They feel confused and overwhelmed.

Questioner : The husband says, "The wife has to compromise. I won't."

Dadashri : Yes, it means everything has reached the limit. If the husband says he will not compromise, but the wife has to, it means he has reached the end of his limit. A real man will respond in a manner that will please his wife and smooth things over so their train of life can move ahead. But instead, you people hold back your train for days and months on end! That is not acceptable. As long as conflicts continue in the mind of the other person, your difficulties will continue. Therefore, work towards a resolution.

Questioner : How can we tell whether the other party has come to a closure but also what if there is harm in it for them?

Dadashri : That is not your concern; it is theirs. You do not have to consider the other person's welfare. Besides who are you to say what is beneficial for him? How can you ascertain what is good for him when you cannot even ascertain what is beneficial for you? People evaluate benefits to the best of their ability. You must keep in mind what is good for others, but only to a certain degree, and if conflicts arise as a result, then it is not acceptable.

Questioner : What should we do when we know that despite our efforts to compromise to reach a settlement with the other person, the outcome is going to be bad?

Dadashri : The outcome may be anything. All you have to do is to have the intent to resolve conflicts with that person. Make a decision to settle with equanimity without worrying whether you will be successful or not. Sooner or later, it will happen; if not today, then tomorrow or the day after; it may even take several years depending on how sticky your karmic account is. The relationships that you have with your wife, children and parents are very sticky and therefore they take longer to settle with equanimity. With those who are always close by or who are always with you, things will resolve slowly and gradually. Once you have decided that you want to settle all accounts with equanimity, it will happen, and there will come an end to it all. You have to maintain extreme awareness when dealing with those, with whom you have very sticky karmic accounts. No matter how small a snake is, you must proceed with caution, maintain awareness. If you become careless and inattentive, you will not be successful in resolving these matters. If the other person says something to you and you happen to retort, your external response is of no significance, because your inner intent now is that you want to settle matters with equanimity, and therefore abhorrence no longer exists. Speech belongs to the body and hatred exists because it is supported by your ego. But, if you decide that you want to settle everything with equanimity, then you will succeed for sure; this way all karmic debts will be cleared. If today you are not able to pay him, you will be able to pay him tomorrow or some time in the future. However, your creditors will eventually collect from you.

After people pay off their karmic debts, upon death, nature strips them of all their worldly possessions. One way or another, debts incurred in the previous life get paid off in this life, but new debts created during this life, remain outstanding for payment in the next life. Now, after having acquired *Gnan* you will not bind any new debts and the old ones will be paid off. Once paid off, you will depart, but if anything remains pending, you will have to spend a few more days clearing it up. The karmic debt for this life is paid off through your current body and the conflicts and mistakes that you make in this life, will be carried forward to the next life, where you will start all over again.

Therefore Avoid Conflicts

Therefore, avoid conflict wherever you can. Conflicts not only ruin your current life, but also the coming one. That which ruins this life is bound to ruin the next. Your next life will improve if your current life improves. If you do not experience any difficulties in your current life then know that you will not have difficulties in your next life. But, if you create difficulties in this life, then they will follow you into your next life.

Questioner : What happens if we create a conflict within a conflict?

Dadashri : Your head will explode! One man asked me how he should go about crossing this ocean of life. I told him, "Avoid conflicts!" He then asked me what I meant by 'conflicts'. So, I asked him what he would do if while walking, he came across a lamppost, would he walk around it or walk into it? If there were a boulder obstructing your path, what would you do? You would walk around it. What would you do if you met a bull on the way? You would have to go around him too; otherwise, the damage would be tremendous if it were to head-butt with you. So, you have to do the same if you come across such people in your life. Conflicts are like that. If someone comes to fight with you and he shouts all kinds of abuse, you must maintain the awareness that you have to avoid conflict. If your mind is still and peaceful, and suddenly something affects it, you must understand right away that the effect is coming from the other person's mind and therefore you should move away from there. There are conflicts everywhere and as your understanding of conflicts increases, you will be able to avoid them. Liberation is attainable by avoiding conflicts. Conflict is the nature of this world. It is in the form of vibrations.

In 1951, I told a man who worked for me to take two words from me: "Avoid Conflicts." I was reading some scriptures and he came to me and said me, "Dada give me something." I asked him, "What can I give you? You cannot get along with anyone. You fight with everyone." I knew that he squandered away all his money and when it came to paying for train fares, he would cheat or not pay enough, on the contrary he would fight with the railway staff. I knew everything about him. So I told him, "You should avoid all conflicts. You do not need to learn anything else." Even to this day, he lives by this command. If you were to pick a fight with him now or call him names or try to provoke him in any way, he will avoid the situation all together.

Avoid conflicts. Conflict is the foundation of the worldly life and its perpetual cycle. God has said that this foundation has been built out of vengeance. Every man, every living being harbors vengeance as a reaction to conflict. If interactions go beyond the limits, then vengeance will surface. Whatever the embodied soul, whether it is a snake, a scorpion, a cow or a bull, they harbor vengeance. This is because every living being has a Soul within and the power of the Soul is the same in every living being. It is because of the body complex weakness (the relative-self) that one has to tolerate suffering and when a person experiences suffering, he cannot help but harbor enmity and that enmity will avenge itself in the next life.

Tolerate? No, Find a Solution

Questioner : Dada, when you tell us to avoid conflict, does that mean we have to tolerate everything?

Dadashri : Avoiding conflict does not mean having to tolerate, and if you do, how much and for how long will you tolerate? Tolerance is like compressing a spring; how long can it remain compressed? Rather than tolerating, you must find a solution.

In the absence of *Gnan* people have no choice but to tolerate everything. However, when one day that 'spring' breaks free of the load it is bearing, it will topple everything in sight; that is the principle of nature.

There is no law of nature that says you have to be tolerant. Whatever you have to tolerate because of someone, is really your own karmic account. But, you do not have the knowledge of past accounts and that is why it appears to you that the other person is dishing out something new; you perceive him as the doer. Nobody is dishing out anything new. They are simply returning what was dished out to them. Our *Gnan* does not require you to tolerate anything. With the application of this *Gnan*, you simply have to realize that the other person is a pure Soul (*Shuddhatma*) and that whatever has come your way is solely because of your own past karma and that the other person is simply an instrument in the process. With this understanding and this *Gnan*, all your puzzles will be solved.

Questioner : Does that mean we have to accept and come to a closure in our mind, that whatever we had dished out is coming back to us?

Dadashri : The other person is a pure Soul and this, on the outside, is his *prakruti*. It is the *prakruti* that delivers the effect of past causes. You are the pure Soul and he too is a pure soul. Now where is the wire that connects the two? This is your *prakruti* and that is his; both the *prakrutis* are settling each other's karmic debts. It is because of the unfolding of this *prakruti's* karma that the other *prakruti* is giving something back. That is why we say, "This is my own karmic account that has come into maturation, the other person is merely instrumental in the process and by doing what he did, my karmic account is cleared and paid off." When you have such a solution, is there a need to tolerate anything at all?

What happens if you try to tolerate? If you do not solve things through *Gnan* and understanding, the spring will one day recoil. Have you ever seen a spring recoil? My spring used to recoil a lot. For a while, I used to tolerate a lot, but then when the 'spring' recoiled, everything around me would blow up! All this used to happen in the absence of *Gnan* but I do remember it well. It is all in my *Gnan* and that is why I am telling you not to learn to tolerate things. It is only in the state of ignorance of the Self that one has to tolerate. You must clarify everything through *Gnan* and understand what the consequences will be by doing things a certain way. What was the cause behind it? You have to look deeper in your account book, not a single event that comes to you is outside of your account book.

Prevention of New Karma

Questioner : How can we prevent a new cycle of this giving and taking for the coming life?

Dadashri : What is the definition of creating a new give-and-take? The causes of karma are the new give-and-take. All that you experience in this life is an effect of causes created in your previous life. Everything that takes place is an effect and the causes are invisible. You cannot see the causes through your senses; whatever you see is all an effect. Therefore, you should realize that your debts are being paid off. Whatever new causes that are being created, are taking place from within, and those you cannot see. You will see them when they produce their results as an effect. The current causes have not yet been transferred to your final ledger.

Questioner : Is all that unfolds today, the account from the final ledger of the past life?

Dadashri : Yes.

Questioner : The conflicts that take place, are they on the basis of *vyavasthit*?

Dadashri : Yes, conflicts occur on the basis of *vyavasthit,* but when can you say that? You can only say it is *vyavasthit* after it happens. Your firm determination must be, "I do not want to get into any conflicts." When you see a pole in your path, your determination is not to walk into it; you know you have to go around it but despite all this, if you still happen to walk into it, then it is *vyavasthit*. However to claim everything is *vyavasthit* ahead of time, is a misuse of it.

For Justice, the Solution Is Penance

Questioner : What should we do if we want to avoid

conflict and settle matters with equanimity, but the other person keeps harassing and insulting us?

Dadashri : Nothing. That is your karmic account and therefore you should make a decision that you want to settle with equanimity. You should remain within the confines of your principles and intentions and continue to solve your own puzzle yourself.

Questioner : When someone insults me, is it because of my ego that I feel insulted?

Dadashri : When someone insults you, he is actually dissolving your ego, and that is your dramatic ego (the relative or discharge ego). Whatever excess ego you may have, becomes dissolved when someone insults you. What harm is it going to cause you? These kinds of karmas prevent your freedom. Even if there is a small child in front of you, you have to tell him to free you.

If someone does injustice to you and you wonder and question why, then you will bind karma. It is on account of your mistake that he has to render the injustice to you. How can one's understanding reach this level? On the contrary, people will cause havoc. In the eyes of God, no one is doing justice or injustice; everything is simply 'correct'. How can one's understanding reach this level? If differences in opinion at home become less, there will be less quarreling and consequently, love will increase amongst everyone. If this happens, then know that *Gnan* has been understood and not otherwise.

Gnan says that you are foolish to look for justice. Penance is the solution for that.

In God's eyes, if someone does you injustice, it is correct. The world on the other hand, will say that he did wrong.

This nature is just. Its justice is not false. It is so precise that not even a single mosquito can touch you, and if it does, then know that there must be a cause behind it, otherwise not a single vibration will touch you. You are completely free. No one can cause any obstructions for you.

Questioner : Is it beneficial to remain silent during a quarrel?

Dadashri : Silence is very beneficial.

Questioner : But Dada, we may be quiet on the outside, but what about the commotion that takes place within?

Dadashri : Then it is of no use; first and foremost, the mind must remain quiet.

The Best Approach is to Adjust Everywhere

Questioner : Do conflicts occur because of the difference in nature of the individual?

Dadashri : The definition of worldly life is conflicts. Wherever there are conflicts, there is worldly life.

Questioner : What is the cause of conflicts?

Dadashri : Ignorance.

Questioner : It is not just my boss that I have conflicts with; I have conflicts with a lot of other people. What about that?

Dadashri : Yes, they will occur with everyone. It may happen with this wall too.

Questioner : What is the solution for that?

Dadashri : I will show you the way so that you will not have any problems, even with a wall. Whose fault is it when you

walk into a wall? The fault is of the one who suffers. What does
the wall have to do with it? It is your fault when you slip and
fall in slippery mud. The mud is just instrumental in the process;
you have to recognize that it is slippery and walk with extra
caution. Mud will always be there and slipperiness is its nature.

Questioner : But what is the reason behind all the
bickering and discord? Is it because of the differences in
personalities?

Dadashri : It is because of ignorance. The very base of
the worldly life is that no two personalities match. The only
solution is to acquire this knowledge: Adjust everywhere. You
have to adjust even when someone hits you.

Questioner : I have a lot of conflicts with my wife and
I am tired of it.

Dadashri : People not only tire from it, but some also
resort to drinking and some even jump into the sea!

What is the greatest suffering of all? It is the suffering that
stems from the inability to adjust. What is wrong in practicing
the principle of, 'adjust everywhere' in such situations?

Questioner : For that, we need to make an effort.

Dadashri : No effort is needed. All you have to do is
follow my *agna*. Tell yourself, "Dada has told me to, 'Adjust
everywhere,'" and then continue to do so. If your wife says,
"You are a thief," then tell her she is correct. Then after a while
if she says, "No you have not stolen anything," then again tell
her she is correct.

The reality is that your entire lifespan is equivalent to only
just one day of *Brahma* (Creator in Hindu mythology). If you
are to live just one day of *Brahma*, then why create all this
commotion? If you were to live a hundred years of *Brahma*,

then it is understandable if you question why you should have to adjust. On the contrary, you can challenge your opponents to file claims against you. But we are talking about just one day of *Brahma* and so you have to resolve everything in a short time. If you have to accomplish a task in a short time, what must you do? Resolve it quickly by adjusting. Otherwise, will it not drag on?

When you fight with your wife, are you able to sleep well at night? No, and the next morning you do not even get a good breakfast.

I have made a very subtle discovery of this worldly life. I am telling you everything having discovered the ultimate truth. I will show you the way to live your daily life and I will also show you how to achieve liberation. My only intent is to minimize your difficulties.

Become a 'Useless Coin'

You should not enforce your control at home. Those who do will have to wander around, life after life. I had told Hiraba that I was a 'useless coin'. Why? I cannot afford to wander life after life. Where does a useless coin end up? He simply has to sit next to God. If you try to exercise control at home, will conflicts not arise? From now on, you must simply settle matters with equanimity. At home, you have to live with your wife as her friend, and she has to do the same. No one cares who is in control, whether it is you or her, and neither is it recorded anywhere in the government books. God does not care either. Are you concerned about the control issue or whether you get food to eat? Therefore only worry and figure out what is the best way to get your meals, don't worry about anything else. I admit I too would not adjust if someone were keeping tract over the issue of control, but in reality nobody cares.

If your feet are hurting and your wife is massaging them, and someone comes along and happens to witness this, he will say, "Wow! You really are the boss at home," you should reply, "No, she is the one with control," because if you say you are in control, she will stop massaging!

Questioner : Is that not flattering her?

Dadashri : No this is the right way; all other ways are crooked and wrong. In the current time cycle, this is a different way to be happy. What I am telling you is applicable only to the current time cycle. Why should you ruin your breakfast and your meals for the entire day?

Do Not Provoke a Reaction

Questioner : By the afternoon, we forget our morning conflicts and the same thing starts over again in the evening.

Dadashri : Yes, I know this. I have the understanding and the knowledge of the power that causes conflicts to arise. I know the power that makes us say the wrong things and the adjustments we take after that. It is possible to understand everything through *Gnan*, and having said that, we must adjust to this world. Everything in this world eventually comes to an end. However, if certain events seem to linger, you do not help matters by reacting, on the contrary, you make matters worse. When that happens, not only are you hurting others, but you are also hurting yourself. Who has the power to improve things? Only the one who have improved himself can improve others. How can you improve others if you, yourself have not?

Questioner : But we can improve others if we improve ourselves, right?

Dadashri : Yes, you can.

Questioner : How can I tell whether I have improved?

Dadashri : When others see love in you even when you reprimand and scold them. Even if you reprimand your child, he will see love in you. You can reprimand your children, but do so with love, only then will they improve. If a college professor were to reprimand his students, they would beat him up.

Your efforts should be aimed for the betterment of the other person, but any effort that causes a reaction, should be avoided. If you rebuke someone and he or she feels bad, then that effort is not worthy. Your efforts should be made from within, in a subtle manner. If your overt efforts are futile, you should make the efforts from within. If you do not want to reprimand at length, then do so in few words Just tell him, "Son this does not suit us (as a family).'" Say only this much and then keep quiet. You have to say something, but you must know the proper way to say it.

Otherwise, Adjust With a Prayer

Questioner : I made my effort to make the other person understand. Whether he understands or not, is it not his *purushartha* (effort)?

Dadashri : The extent of your responsibility is to explain things to him. After that, whether or not he understands, there is nothing you can do. At the very least, you should do this much. You should pray, "Dada Bhagwan (the Lord within)! Grant him the right intellect." You cannot leave that person hanging. This is the absolute truth; this is Dada's science of adjustment. It is a wonderful adjustment. Do you not get the taste of the consequences wherever you fail to adjust? Inability to adjust is sheer foolishness, it happens because a person believes he is the boss and everything should go according to his plans. For that, he will have to starve his entire life and one day, he may be served with poison. Let things be. This is *Kaliyug*! Just look at the environment! If your wife tells you that you are worthless, you should just say yes.

Questioner : It would provoke me if my wife were to call me worthless.

Dadashri : So what is the solution for it? Should you retaliate and call her worthless twice over? And by doing that will your own worthlessness disappear? By retaliating, you ruin your whole day *and* your meals.

Questioner : What is the intention behind all these talks of adjustment? Where do we go from there?

Dadashri : The aim is to achieve peace of mind. It is the art of avoiding unhappiness and discord.

Learn To Adjust From a *Gnani*

There was a man who used to come home at two in the morning. What he did before he came home is not worthy of discussion. You can figure it out yourself. His whole family was in a dilemma about whether they should reprimand him or not let him in the house. They did not know what to do with him. When the eldest brother tried to confront him, he threatened him saying, "I will not refrain from hurting you." The family then came to me for a solution. I told them not to say a word to him, because it would make matters worse and if they prevented him from coming home, he would resort to stealing. I told him to let him come and go as he pleased. They were not to tell him what was right and what was wrong, nor were they to harbor any feelings of attachment or abhorrence towards him. On the contrary, they were to have compassion for him. After three or four years, he became a changed man. Today he is extremely helpful in the family business. This world is not worthless; you just need to know how to handle situations. God resides in each person. Everyone has his load cut out, so do not have a dislike towards anyone.

Great Injustice in Suppressing those Under Your Shelter

Questioner : I do not get along with my wife at all. No matter what I say, no matter how innocently I say it, and regardless of when I am right, she always takes it the wrong way. There are external conflicts in life, but what is this friction between two of us?

Dadashri : It's like this. People repress those who are under them to a degree that has no end. People who exercise excess authority over others, be it a wife or a husband, stop at nothing.

You should never quarrel with your family members. How can you quarrel with those you have to share your room with? No one has been happy by hurting others. We want to achieve happiness by making others happy. If you give happiness in your home, you will get happiness in return. You will even get a decent breakfast, but otherwise your tea will be ruined. Husbands who intimidate their wives are weak. How can you destroy those who are under your protection? Your highest goal should be to protect those who have been placed in your care. You should protect them even if they make mistakes. These are people of your own family! See how well we protect the Pakistani prisoners of war? Outside the home, he barely squeals and will not fight with anyone, but at home, he will do all kinds of mischief. He keeps suppressing those who are under him and he becomes weak and submissive to his superiors. If a police officer reproaches him, he will say, "Yes sir, yes sir." But at home, even if his wife is right, he cannot bear it and will start yelling at her. "How come there is an ant in my tea?" he will yell at her. You fool! Why can't you calmly remove it from your tea? He tyrannizes those at home but he trembles in front of a police officer. This is gross injustice and it does not suit us. Your wife is your partner. How can you fight with your partner? Wherever there is a potential for a conflict, you must be understanding and find a solution. Why do you have conflicts with people you have to live with?

A Science Worth Understanding

Questioner : What should we do if we do not want to get into a conflict but the other person comes to pick a fight? Say one is very careful and aware, and the other is bent on fighting, is conflict not inevitable?

Dadashri : How long can a person fight with a wall? If you were to run into a wall, what should you do to it? Should you fight with it? Similarly, those with whom you come into conflict are walls. What should you do in that situation? Recognize and accept they are walls. Then there will be no problems.

Questioner : If we remain silent, the other person may mistake our silence as admission of our guilt and in turn fight even harder.

Dadashri : This is your belief only. If a man gets up to go to the bathroom in the night and bumps into the wall, does that mean that the wall bumped into him because he remained silent?

Whether you say something or not has no bearing on anything. It is not true that your silence has any effect on the other person and neither is it true that your speech has any effect. Everything is simply interplay of scientific circumstantial evidences. No one has even the slightest authority or power in this world, so who is going to get away with anything? If this wall had the power to do anything, then so would the body. Do we have the authority or the power to fight with this wall? In the same way, what is the point of getting angry and fighting with people? The other person definitely does not have the independent control or power, so why don't you also become like the wall? When you scold your wife, the God within her makes a note of what you are doing. If she starts to scold you, you should become like the wall, and the God within you will help you.

Fault Is Of the Sufferer

Questioner : Some people just do not understand, no matter how nicely you interact with them.

Dadashri : If they do not understand, then the fault is yours. Why did you get such a person with limited understanding? Why is it that only you had to have an encounter with such a person? Anytime you have to suffer, know that it is the consequence of your own mistakes.

Questioner : So do I have to accept that such is my own karma?

Dadashri : Definitely. If there is no mistake on your part, you will not have to suffer anything. There is nobody in this world that can hurt you in the slightest but if someone does, then it is because of your own mistake. The other person is simply instrumental in the process of your own unfolding karma. Therefore, the fault is of the sufferer.

A husband and wife get into a big row with each other and then retire to bed. The wife is sleeping soundly and snores while the husband tosses and turns in bed. Understand that the husband is the one at fault because he is the one suffering, not the wife. The one who is at fault is the one who suffers. If he falls asleep and the wife cannot, then recognize that she is the one at fault. Fault is of the sufferer.

This science is extraordinary. What I am telling you is a very subtle science. The whole world blames only the apparent doer (*nimit*).

Husband – Wife

This world is very vast but people do not perceive it that way. For some, their home is the entire world to them. There is nothing wrong in thinking that way, but even in his home, he fights with his wife. You fool she is not your enemy.

When husband and wife fight with the neighbors, they are united. If you see them, you would think their unity is praiseworthy and admirable, but inside the house, if the wife does not put enough sugar in his tea, he starts lecturing her, "Every day, I tell you to put more sugar in the tea but your mind is never in the right place." You fool! Your own mind is not in the right place. What kind of a man are you anyway? Should you be quarrelling with the person with whom you have ongoing interactions everyday?

Do you have differences of opinions with anyone?

Questioner : Yes, a lot of times.

Dadashri : Do you have differences of opinions with your wife?

Questioner : Yes, many times.

Dadashri : Even with your wife? If you cannot be united with her, then with whom can you be? Unity means never having differences of opinions. Your wife is the one person with whom you must vow never to have any differences. That is how united you should be. Do you have such a unity?

Questioner : I have never thought about it this way before. This is the first time I am thinking this way.

Dadashri : Yes, you will have to think, will you not? Do you know how much thinking Lord (Mahavira) did before his final liberation? Do you like having differences?

Questioner : No.

Dadashri : Differences of opinions lead to fights and worries. If that happens because of differences in opinions then imagine what would happen if there are differences amongst the minds? When that happens, divorces take place and when there is a difference with the body, death will occur.

Fight, But In the Park

If you want to fight, go outside and do it. Make that your rule. The day the two of you want to fight, go to a park and fight as much as you want, then come home, but do not fight at home. The day you feel like fighting with your wife, tell her, "Let us go to a park and have a nice picnic and then we can fight to our heart's content." Fight in a way that others will get involved. There should be no fighting at home. God does not reside in a home where there is discord. What has God said? He has said there should be no fighting in the home of a devotee. A devotee is anyone whose worship is indirect (*paroksha bhakti*) through the medium of a picture, an image, an idol etc. And a devotee whose worship is direct, (*pratyaksha*), one who has the awareness and the realization of the Soul within is called a *'Gnani'*, and there can be no conflicts in the home of a *Gnani*, only eternal bliss (*samadhi*) prevails there.

So if someday you have a desire to fight, tell your husband, "Let's go to the park." Send the children to someone else. Then tell your husband to smile when you slap him in public. Let the public witness your drama. People are big on impressions. When they see you both, they will think to themselves, "Here is a man who is very honorable, but today he has no reputation left." Does anyone have any honor left today? People create a reputation for themselves by hiding the truth.

Attachment : *Moha*

A man of reputation looks wonderful even when he walks around without clothes. People today do not look good even when they wear good clothes. A man looks like a bull even in a suit and a tie. He thinks he is someone special. He does not even accept other people's opinion. He doesn't even ask his wife if he looks good in a suit and a tie. He looks in the mirror and decides that he looks good. The wife does the same thing as she looks at herself and moves her head in the mirror. What is all this? What kind of a life is this? You are God so what is all this nonsense? The real you is God.

Women wear earrings in their ears, but can they even to see them? They wear diamonds in their ears to show others. They are trapped in worldly entanglement and yet they go around showing off their diamonds. Alas, can someone trapped in a web of entanglement afford to have desires? Why do you not get out of it and find a solution as fast as you can? You can wear your earrings if your husband asks you. If a man buys a pair of earring worth two thousand rupees, but the bill shows thirty-five thousand rupees, his wife will be very flattered. What is the point when she cannot even see them when she wears them? I asked one such lady if she could see her earrings in her sleep at night. This is all projected and imagined happiness. People have a wrong belief about what happiness is and that is why they have no inner peace. Whom can you call a woman of India? A woman of India is one who will wear a two thousand-rupee sari while sitting at home. However, when a couple goes shopping, the wife sees an embroidered sari worth one thousand rupees in the window. This sari has such a hold over her that even when she goes home, she is in a foul mood and picks a fight with everyone. How can you call someone like her a woman of India?

Hindu Husbands Are Weak

Hindus, by their very nature have a propensity towards conflict. That is why it is said that Hindus spend their lives in conflict. Muslims on the other hand, are smart. They fight outside of their homes but they will not fight with their wives at home. Some Muslims however, have become like the Hindus by living with them, but to me, in these matters, the Muslims are still better than the Hindus. Some Muslim men pamper their wives a lot. As a contractor, I used to visit many Muslim homes and have tea with them. I did not have any prejudices. One day I visited one such home and to my surprise, the man started to push the swing on which his wife was sitting. So, I asked him, "Does she not take advantage of you when you pamper her this way?" He replied, "How is she going to take advantage of me? She does not have any weapon to do so." I told him, "Our Hindu men do nothing of the sort because they are afraid their wives will take advantage of them." He then asked me if I knew why he was pampering his wife. He told me, "We do not have a bungalow; we have only these two rooms to live in, so if I fight with my wife, where would I go to sleep? My whole night would be ruined. So I just fight with everyone outside the home but with my wife, I keep everything clear." If he comes home empty-handed when the wife had asked him to buy some meat, he promptly tells he will buy some the next day. Then the next morning he tells her, "I promise I will get some meat today from wherever I can," and yet he returns home empty-handed. His wife gets annoyed with him but he knows how to pacify her, "My dearest only I know what I am going through," and he somehow manages to appease her with his smooth talk, but he will not get into an argument with her. Whereas what do the Hindu men do? They will say, "You keep pressuring me. You are trying to control me. I am not going to get it." You fools! You cannot talk this way, by doing so you lose your worthiness.

When you talk this way, it really shows that you are the one that is weak and inferior. How can she be controlling you? Just remain silent when she speaks. Only the weak get annoyed easily. So, when she gets annoyed, you should remain silent and just listen to her 'record'.

If a Muslim man is unhappy with his wife's cooking and makes a comment about it and the wife gets angry, he will then remain silent and not say anything to antagonize her because he knows that if he does, the situation will blow up. He will mind his own business and let her mind hers, whereas the Hindu men will not refrain from blowing up the situation.

Every cast and creed wears its hats differently. The *Vanik* (traders) has his own hat, the *Brahmin* has his hat; each has his own way of wearing it. Everyone is different. Everyone's viewpoint is different and therefore, they cannot agree upon things, but it is best if quarrels do not arise.

Be Vigilant Before Differences Arise

If there is no intent of hostility left within you, then the other person will not have any intent of hostility towards you either. If you do not get annoyed or angry, neither will they. You have to become like a brick wall so that you hear nothing. Hiraba and I have been married for fifty years but we have never had any differences. If Hiraba spills *ghee*, I simply watch. My knowledge that she is not the one spilling is present at the time. Even if I ask her to spill, she will not. Would anyone spill anything valuable on purpose? No. Therefore, when *ghee* spills, you should just observe it. Before any conflicts arise, this *Gnan* is present on-the-moment.

A wife is easily pacified if the husband tells her, "Only I know what I am going through," but our Hindu men do not even say that; at least say this much so that happiness prevails.

When you got married, it was in the presence of Suryanarayan, the Sun God, the priest and guests. The priest was your witness and at that time, you agreed to "Exercise caution according to situations." But, you do not know how to be cautious. You should practice caution as the situation dictates. When the priest chants, *"Samaya varte savdhan,"* (Be cautious as the situation calls for) during the marriage ceremony, he himself understands what that means, but does the groom? What does it mean? It means that when the wife gets upset, you should maintain caution, be very careful. Would the neighbors not come to watch if the two of you were to fight, and make a spectacle of yourselves? If you were never going to get back together again then go ahead and fight, but why do you fight otherwise? Should you not have this understanding and awareness?

A female trait is such that she will never change and therefore you will have to. Women are spontaneous (*sahaj*) in nature, and therefore not likely to change.

Say your wife gets upset and says, "I am not bringing you a plate of food upstairs anymore; you will have to come down and get it yourself. You are now well and able. You wander around and gossip with people, you smoke cigarettes, but when it is time for you to eat, you ask me to bring your plate up to you. I am not going to do that." That is when you must say to her calmly, "Please fix me the plate, and I will come down and get it myself." Even before she has a chance to say anything, just tell her that you are sorry and that you are coming. If you do this, you will sleep peacefully. Otherwise, your entire night will be ruined. Both of you will pout, you will sleep separately and not sleep well, and then in the morning, she will still be sulking when she serves you your breakfast. You will notice it right away. This life is full of conflicts and quarrels. The Hindus spend their whole life in conflicts and quarrels.

A Home Without Conflict, Is A Temple

God does not reside in a home where there are conflicts. Therefore tell God, "Sir, stay in the temple, do not come to our home. We will build temples for you but do not come to our home." I assure you that God resides in a home where there is no conflict. Conflicts can be destroyed through understanding and intellect. Even through your *prakruti*, without Self-realization, you can have the understanding of how to avoid conflicts caused by difference in opinions. This is done through the medium of the right intellect. True understanding exists when there remain no differences with anyone. Differences occur because communication is inadequate and ineffective. Otherwise, there would be no differences in opinions. These differences of opinions are the cause of conflict; it is a weakness.

When any conflict occurs, if you take time and calm down, and let you *chit* (inner organ of knowledge and vision) simmer down, and then analyze the situation by thinking about it, you will experience inner clarifications and understanding. God will leave your home as soon as there is a quarrel, will he not?

Questioner : Yes, he would.

Dadashri : God will not leave people's homes but when quarrel arises, He will say, "Let us go from here, we will not be comfortable here," and so God leaves for the *derasars* (Jain temples) and the temples. People quarrel and steal from temples also, and so God says, "Let us leave from here too." Even God has become tired of all this.

You should have a conflict-free life at home. You should at least know how to attain that. If you do not know anything else, at least explain to your family in this way: "God will leave if there are conflicts and quarrels in our home. Therefore, let us decide that we do not want any conflicts." You should make a decision that you do not want to quarrel. If quarrels occur in spite of this decision, then realize that it is beyond your control. If he starts to quarrel, just pull the blanket over your head and go to sleep. After a while, he too will go to sleep. But, what happens if you start to answer back?

The Curse of Dishonest Money

In Bombay, I asked the lady of a very reputable family if she had quarrels in her home. She replied, "We have quarrels for breakfast every morning." I said, "Then you must be saving money on food!" She replied, "No, we still have to eat breakfast." Therefore, they quarrel and have breakfast. What kind of creatures are these people of today?

Questioner : Does the quarreling have anything to do with the kind of money people have?

Dadashri : That is the very cause. If the money is pure, the mind will always remain pure. The wealth that has entered the home has been acquired through dishonest means and that is why it creates quarrels. That is why I had decided from a very young age that if possible, I did not want any illicit money entering my home and if it did under certain circumstances, then it should be left in the business and should not enter the home at all. It has been sixty-six years and not a single penny of illicit money, has entered my home and never has a conflict arisen in the home. From the very beginning, we had decided that we would run the household within a certain budget. The business may make a profit of thousands of rupees but how much money would A. M. Patel make if he were to work for someone else? At the most, he would earn six hundred to seven hundred rupees a month. Success in business depends on the merit karma. Our spending was limited to the amount of salary I would have earned as an employee and the rest of the money was left in the business. If the income tax office were to write to the business asking for money, I would just have to instruct them to pay off the debt from the money retained in the business. One can never tell what kind of an attack may come. Now if the money had all been spent, then an attack from the income tax office, will lead to a heart attack! Have we not seen these attacks come to people? How can you call this a life? What do you think? Do you think it is a mistake or not? This is the mistake that you have to destroy.

At Least Try the Experiment

At least decide that you do not want any conflicts. Do this for three days; what's wrong in trying the experiment? People experiment with fasting, they'll fast for three days for their health, so why not try this? Everyone in the household should get together and decide, "We like what Dada is saying. Let us all make a decision to do away with conflicts." Do this and see what happens.

Religion Means No Conflicts

Wherever there is no conflicts and discord, there is the exact religion (*dharma*) of the Jain, the Vaishnav, and the Shaivite. Since there are conflicts in every home, where have all these religions gone?

If a person learns the art of living, whereby it reduces all conflicts from his worldly life, then it can be said that he has attained religion.

True *dharma* is to live life without conflicts. In India, only if one's own home becomes like heaven, can one even begin to talk about liberation, but not otherwise. The home may not be like heaven but at least it should come close to being one!

Your life should become free of conflicts. The home

environment must be free from conflicts. Only then should one talk of liberation, not otherwise. Leaving aside the state of total freedom from conflicts, one should experience at least some freedom from conflicts. That is why the scriptures say, "Where there is the slightest of conflict, there is no religion." Inner harmony means no feelings of depression or elevation. No depression in the jail and no elevation in a palace. If your life becomes free of conflicts, know that you have come closer to liberation. You should feel some peace here and now. Everyone wants liberation because no one likes to be bound. When your life becomes free of conflicts, your liberation is close by.

Mend When You Are Hurt By Others

I asked a *Vania* (business sect in Gujarat who are apt in human interactions) man if he had conflicts in his home. "Many times," he told me. I asked him what his solution to them was. "First I close my front door and then we fight," he replied. I then asked what his reason was for closing the door. I inquired. He went on, "If people get into the house, they will prolong the conflict. If we fight amongst ourselves, things will calm down soon." This man's intellect was good. I liked that. If people have even this much intelligence, we have to accept it. Otherwise, a dunce will open his door and invite people in to see. The foolish man! Doing that is called a *'taipho'* (deliberately involving others in a personal conflict by complaining profusely. This is a devious ploy people use to get what they want).

When you get into conflict with people, no one but yourself will be held responsible. In such situations, you will have to extricate yourself. If you are truly a wise man, then just continue mending, even if the other person keeps breaking. This will free you. The very nature of people is to exacerbate conflicts. If you have attained the Self and if people do you wrong, just make it right; do not rebel against them or their

actions. People do things that make no sense. They will put the
bucket upside down and leave the tap running all night long.
They only ruin things for themselves; they think they are ruining
things for the other person, but this can never be. No one is
capable of ruining anything for anyone else. No such person has
been born.

It is impossible to assess the *prakrutis* of Indian people.
God himself becomes baffled! The *prakruti* of people in other
countries is straightforward. For example, if a man vows to
remain faithful to his wife, then he will do so for the rest of his
life. But here, you can observe a person's *prakruti* all daylong
and still not be able to assess it. Their karmas and *prakruti* are
very complex. Their unfolding karmas drive them to do things
that put them at a disadvantage and they hurt themselves.
Otherwise, are these people likely to do anything that would
cause them hurt? Not these people, they are extremely shrewd.
They would be cautious even when they are dying, they would
put their soul aside and then die!

Resolve Conflicts by Turning Your Words Around

Dadashri : Do you have conflicts when you are having
your meals?

Questioner : Conflicts are inevitable, Dada.

Dadashri : Why? Did you make a contract to do that
when you got married?

Questioner : No.

Dadashri : At the time of your wedding, you agreed to
be aware and maintain awareness when times called for it. In
your home, you should not use words like, 'mine' and 'yours'.
Your speech should not create a separation; do you not belong
to a family that never divides?

I had never had any differences of opinions with Hiraba; never had there been speech between us using words such as 'mine' or 'yours', but one day, we had a little difference of opinion. Hiraba's brother's eldest daughter was getting married, so she asked me what we should give her as a wedding gift. I told her, "Give whatever you want but we already have some silverware at home, why do not you give her that? Do not give an order to the goldsmith for new silver plates." To that, she responded, "When girls from your mother's family get married, you give special orders for big silver plates!" In this event, she used the words 'mine' and 'yours'. I immediately understood that I had lost my reputation, I understood that we two were one, so where did this 'mine' and 'yours' come from? I understood right away and immediately turned things around; I told her "That's not what I am saying. What I meant was that you can give her the silverware and also give her five hundred rupees; they can use the money." She immediately responded, "Huh! How can you give so much money? You are so naive in every situation. You give money to every Tom, Dick and Harry that comes along." I told her, "I truly do not know anything."

Just look at how I turned everything around to prevent a conflict between us! The bottom line is that I did not allow any differences of opinions to take place between us. For the last thirty to thirty-five years, we have had no conflicts between us and before any conflicts can take place, I know how to turn things around. You only know of a few ways to avoid conflicts, whereas I have endless keys and solutions. I resolve all matters at hand, without allowing any conflicts to occur. There are some twenty thousand people in our *satsang*, of which about four thousand are *mahatmas*, the ones who have taken *Gnan*, but I do not have any conflict or differences of opinions with any of them. I have never considered myself as being separate or different from anyone. I maintain oneness with everyone.

Where there is a difference of opinion, there is partial *gnan* and in the absence of conflicts, there is absolute science, *Gnan*. Where there is science, there is absolute knowledge. Only if you remain in the center, in your absolute state as the Self, there will be no conflicts and only then will you attain liberation. If you move away from the center, there will be differences of 'mine' and 'yours' and liberation cannot be attained. Only the impartial one will be liberated.

What are the signs of being enlightened? It is when everyone in the home does wrong and you turn it around and make it right. All you have to know is how to fix the fuse on a machine if it blows up. You must know how to adjust with people's *prakruti*. For me, even when the other person blows his fuse, my adjustment is always there. But, what happens when the other person does not know how to adjust? He loses his fuse and gets into a conflict with everyone until someone fixes his fuse, but until then his confusion remains.

In this worldly life, wounds are inevitable. Even the women of the household will say, "This hurt will not heal, enough is enough." But once she is drawn back into the worldly life, the wounds heal. Because of the attachment for the worldly life, the illusion continues. That which is not real, appears real. Therefore, the wounds heal. The allure for worldly things and life continues. If the wounds did not heal, then renunciation of worldly life would grow. What is the definition of attachment (*moha*)? It is where a person tolerates many painful experiences but then forgets them all. For example, when a man goes through a divorce he resolves he will never get involved with another woman, and then he marries again.

What a Trap!

How will this world maintain a balance if people won't

get married? Go ahead and get married, it is perfectly fine to do so. Dada has no objection to that, but the problem is with your incorrect and incomplete understanding. What I am saying is you can do everything, but at least understand the reality of this world.

Emperor Bharat had thirteen hundred queens! He spent his entire life with them and yet attained liberation in the same lifetime. Thirteen hundred wives! So all you have to do is understand the matter. Live your worldly life with an understanding. You do not have to become an ascetic. If you do not understand, then become a hermit and live in isolation. Otherwise, the life of a hermit is only meant for the one who cannot get along with a woman; it is an exercise to test one's willpower to see if he can stay away from women.

The worldly life is an examination; it is a test. You are being tested in it, and you have to pass the test. When even iron has to be tested as a metal, is it any different for achieving *moksha*?

You cannot afford to remain in this illusion. It is because of this illusion (*moha*; *maya*) that you perceive the world the way you do. This is why you suffer. Imagine the state of Emperor Bharat having to deal with thirteen hundred wives! Even when there is just one queen at home, she creates such a scene, so just imagine what it would be like with thirteen hundred of them! Alas even with one queen (wife), life is a challenge; you can never win! Once you have a difference of opinion, you are stuck! Bharat had to tolerate thirteen hundred of them. As he passed through the queens' palaces, fifty of them would be smiling, while many of them were plotting against him. Their jealousy towards other queens drove them to plot against Emperor Bharat; all this to take revenge on the Emperor's current favorite queen. Their hatred was for the queen yet they plotted against the King. It is of no consequence to them that they too would become widows; they just wanted to make sure that the favorite queen became a widow!

I can see very clearly the scenario of Emperor Bharat and his queens. How the queens were sulking; how the king agonized worrying. I can see it all. On the other hand, if one queen were married to thirteen hundred kings, the kings would not have sulking faces. Men do not know how to sulk.

Accusations – How Hurtful They Are!

Everything is readily available, but people just do not know how to enjoy it. They do not know the art of enjoyment. As the wealthy businessmen sit to dine at their enormous dinning table, they complain and fight with their wives. They complain that their wives do not let them be at peace and that they nag for no reason. Little do they realize that no one can bother anyone else without a reason and a past cause. If someone *does* bother them, it is well within the laws of nature, and yet they go around making such accusations. They have no clue. The human quality is lost. How can anyone accuse members of his own family? People of past time cycle never accused each other, even when they had a reason to. They would first think about the hurt they would inflict through their accusations. But today, in the *Kaliyug*, people scheme to get even. How can it be acceptable to have conflict in one's own home?

The Liability is Your Own When You Clash.

Questioner : What is the reason behind differences in opinions and conflicts?

Dadashri : Terrible ignorance! Man does not know how to live, he does not know how to be a father, nor does he know how to be a husband. He does not know the art of living.

Despite having happiness, people do not know how to enjoy it.

Questioner : But utensils are bound to make a noise!

Dadashri : But how can you live with noisy utensils day in and day out? People continue to live this way because they do not have the understanding. If a person had awareness, he would not be able to sleep at night with a single conflict. These utensils (people) emit vibrations even if they are asleep, "He's like this," and "He's like that." "He is awkward," "He's difficult," "He is unfit," "He should be thrown out." The other (non-living) utensils do not emit any vibrations. People put in their two-bit without understanding; they claim two utensils are bound to make a noise! Listen here you foolish people! Are you a utensil? Do we need to make a noise? No one has ever seen this Dada make noise with anyone. Not even in a dream. Why all the noise? The noise you make is at your own liability, not anyone else's. It is better for you to sit in a corner like an idiot and tell yourself, "It is fine if I get tea for breakfast, if not I'll drink it at the office." What's wrong with doing that? Besides, does tea not have its time also? This world never operates outside the laws of *vyavasthit*. When the time comes, you will get your tea, you will not have to make a noise for it. It will come, whether you create vibrations or not. But in the latter situation, you will create an account with your wife and she will remind you one day that you were banging on the table for your tea!

Understand *Prakruti* and Be Cautious

Men forget events, but women will remember them for the rest of their lives Men are innocent and easygoing, they have generous minds; they are forgiving by nature. Women, on the other hand, will rehash by saying, "That day you said such and such words to me and it really wounded my heart." Alas even after twenty years, her memory is so fresh? Many things will rot but not her memory! Whatever you give to a woman, she will store it in a very appropriate place, her heart; so do not tell her anything! You cannot afford to say anything hurtful and besides nothing is meant for hurting. You have to be very cautious.

That is why it is written in the scriptures, "It is easy to play with a woman, but when she gets upset, you are doomed!" So you cannot keep picking on her, you cannot complain, "Why are the vegetables cold?" or "The *daal* does not have enough salt." Why must you nag so? It is acceptable if you complain once in a while, but for you it is an everyday affair. There is another saying, "If the father-in-law keeps within his boundary, the daughter-in-law will show respect."

You have to maintain your boundaries. If the vegetables are cold or the *daal* does not taste good, it is well within the laws of nature. If you find it unbearable, then you say something like, "These vegetables tasted very good the other day when they were hot." If you say it like this, then she will get the message.

The Uncertified Rider

A man buys a mare for eighteen hundred rupees and tries to sit on her. First of all, he does not know how to sit on a horse and on top of that, he aggravates the horse a little. She has never been needled before so she immediately jolts up in a standing position, throwing the fool to the ground. Then the fool complains to everyone that the horse threw him off. To whom, can the mare defend herself? If you do not know how to sit on her, whose fault is it, yours or hers? The mare too, understands the moment he mounts her, that some untamed animal is getting on and that he does not know how to sit. The women of India are noble and respectable. If you do not know how to deal with them, then naturally they are going to throw you off. If a husband goes against his wife just once, he will lose all his worthiness. Your household is running smoothly, the children are studying well, and there are no problems, but even then, you find faults and complain; you become cantankerous without any reason. When you do this, your wife immediately assesses your intellect, and realizes that you have no substance.

Even if you are not worthy of riding the mare, if you stroke her gently, she will give you her affection. If you can overlook many of your wife's shortcomings or mistakes, then she will be impressed with you, but instead you accuse her of making mistakes when she makes none. Many men complain about issues regarding women's responsibilities and chores; it is all unnecessary. Many bosses are such that they interfere in the clerk's business; the clerks are aware that their boss is mediocre and has no substance but what can anyone do? His merit karma has made him a boss, but at home, he has unresolved quarrels with his wife every fortnight. If someone asks him why he has problems with his wife, he will say, "She has no commonsense," and yet his intellect is such that no one will pay even a dime for it! If we ask his wife, she will say, "What is there to talk about? There is nothing in him worth talking about."

If you hurt a woman's pride, she will never forget it; she will remember it for the rest of her life. The feelings of hurt and resentment will remain alive, up until her funeral. If women could forget their hurt, this world would have come to an end. So beware of the fact that they cannot forget. You have to be cautious about everything you do.

You have heard the term *'stri charitra'* (female behavior), however it is not something that can be understood. What is more, women are also referred to as divine beings. It means that if you regard her as a divine, you will become divine. Otherwise, you remain like a rooster or an elephant. Here comes Mr. Rooster and Mr. Elephant! You men do not want to become like Lord Rama, but you look for a Sita (ideal woman) in your home! You foolish men, Lord Rama would not even employ you! Nevertheless, you are not to be blamed. You just do not know how to deal with women. You businessmen do not even know how to deal with your customers. That is why employing sales people, is a great practice. If you employ a salesman who is good looking and clever, people will even pay a little extra. In the same way, you men should know how to interact with women. On one hand, you must regard her as divine and on the other hand, you must understand her conduct; maintain love in one eye and sternness in the other. Only then will you be able to maintain a balance. If you regard her as divine and put her on a pedestal, she will be led astray, so maintain a balance.

Departments: Husband's & Wife's

The man should not interfere in the woman's affairs and the woman should not interfere in the affairs of the man. Each should remain confined to his or her own departments.

Questioner : What is the woman's department? What should men not interfere in?

Dadashri : Cooking, running the household etc., are women's responsibilities. Why do men need to know where their wives buy the groceries? It is a different matter if she consults you for something, but if not, what possible reason do you have to meddle? Additionally, what is the need for you to tell her what to cook? When the time comes, your dinner will be served. Her department is her own. If at times you crave certain food, you may ask her, "Can you make *ladoos* today?" I am not asking you to remain silent at all times, but you men have a habit of needlessly commenting on the cooking; "There's too much salt in the vegetables," or "There's too little salt," there is no need for that.

Take this railroad for example; there are so many different functions going on, so many signals being fed from so many directions, that it is a department all by itself, and therefore mistakes are inevitable. In the same way, there may be mistakes in your wife's department. But, if you start pointing out these mistakes, she will do the same to you. She will start to complain, "You do not do this," and "You do not do that." She will get even with you. If I were to start pointing out your mistakes, you would do the same to me. A wise man would never interfere in domestic matters; that is a real man! Some men are like women; they go into the kitchen and check all the spice containers. They'll say, "We bought chili powder two months ago and it's already finished?" You fool! If you worry about the chili powder, when will it all end? Don't you think that she knows her responsibilities? Things get used up and you have to buy more, so why must you meddle in it when there is no need? The wife too, will come to know that her husband is not very bright. Just as a horse comes to know the way of its rider, the wife too will come to know all about her husband. It is better that you stick to your turf and she sticks to hers. We have a saying, "If the father-in-law remains in his boundaries, then the daughter-in-law will show her respect." Your interactions will only be ideal if you have principles and limits. Do not cross the boundaries of your limitations; remain pure in these matters.

Questioner : In which of her husband's affairs should the wife not interfere?

Dadashri : She should not interfere in any of his affairs of business. She should not concern herself with how much business he conducts day in and day out. She should not question why he comes home late. Some women question, "Why did you come home late today?" The husband will say he missed the nine o'clock train, so she will make a comment like, "How careless of you that you miss your train!" He will then get irritated and think to himself, "Even if God were to say such things, I would beat him up!" But what can he do here? This is how husband and wife meddle without any reason. It's like putting sand in your tasty basmati rice and eating it. What possible enjoyment can you get eating that rice? Husbands and wives should help each other. A wife should speak with her husband in a manner that will not cause him to worry and the husband should do the same. He should understand how difficult and frustrating children can be when they do not behave. If things break in the home, he should not complain or get angry. Some men make a big fuss over broken crockery or china; they will blame the wife and keep reminding her. The wife in turn retaliates and they will fight over the most insignificant things.

Hiraba and I never have any differences of opinions! I never interfere with anything she does. Even if she happens to drop some money, I will not say to her, "Do you know you've dropped some money?" I never interfere with any domestic matters and she never interferes in any of my business matters. She never questions what time I will wake up, when I will take my bath, or what time I will come home or leave home. Sometimes she tells me to take an early bath and I will do so without questioning her. I will even fetch my own towel and clothes because when she tells me to take an early bath, she is waving a red flag; she must have a reason to do so. Perhaps the water is going to be shut off or something, therefore I understand. You too, should gradually try to understand that no one should interfere in anyone else's business.

If a police officer were to arrest you and take you away, do you not do as you are told? Wouldn't you sit where he told you? You should understand that as long as you are in this world, you are under arrest. So here too, you should do as you are told.

Does your wife cook for you?

Questioner : Yes she does.

Dadashri : She feeds you, she makes your bed, and she does your laundry, what else? And even if she does not make your bed, you can make it yourself and solve the problem. Explain everything patiently. Are you going to find your solutions in the 'Bhagvad Gita'? This is something you will have to understand for yourself.

'Husband' means the wife of the wife! But here, men only act as husbands; as bosses. You fools! Do you fear your wife is going to become your husband? To be a husband means to be a wife of the wife. There should be no loud noises or raised voices in your household; are you a loud speaker? Some husbands speak so loudly that they can be heard at the end of the street! You should live like a guest in your home. I too live like a guest at home. If you do not find happiness as a guest of nature, what happiness do you expect to find in your married life?

She Will Avenge the Beatings

Questioner : Dada, many times I loose my temper and hit my wife.

Dadashri : You should never hit a woman. She will remain silent as long as you are strong, then she will overrule you. Beating a woman and beating the mind are the causes that will make you wander life after life. You can never beat these two. You have to explain things to them and reason with them in order to get your work done.

I had a friend who would slap his wife the minute he saw

her make mistakes. I told him in confidence that she makes a note of every slap she gets. He may not remember anything, but she definitely will. Alas! Even his little children, who watch intently when he hits her, will make a note of it. Then the mother and the children will get together and join forces against him and take their revenge. When will they do this? They will do this when his body becomes old and weak. Therefore, you must never hit a woman. By hitting a woman, you hurt only yourself and create your own obstacles.

Let me tell you what dependency is. If you beat a tethered cow, where can she go? How can she escape the beatings? People in a household are like the tethered cows. If you beat them, you are nothing but a shameless beast. Why don't you untie her and then beat her? She'll hit you back or she will run away. How can you ever call it a noble act if you beat someone who is absolutely helpless? These are the acts of spineless cowards! You can never hurt anyone in your household; only those who have no understanding will do so.

If You Complain, You Are At Fault

Questioner : Dada, who will listen to my complaints?

Dadashri : If you complain, you become the culprit. I regard anyone that comes complaining to me as being the culprit. Why is it that you even have an occasion to complain in the first place? Very often, people who complain are culprits themselves. If you complain, you are the culprit and the person you accuse will become the plaintiff, he will now have a complaint against you. So, never complain about anyone.

Questioner : So what should I do?

Dadashri : If the other person appears wrong to you, you have to tell yourself, "He is the nicest man and I am the one at fault." If you have multiplied your negative opinions about him, then you have to divide them and if you have divided, then you should multiply equally.

I am teaching you to multiply and divide, in order to close all of your worldly accounts. If the other person is dividing then you should multiply in order to zero out the account. If you keep accusing the other person in your mind, then that in itself is a fault on your part. If you are walking along and bump into a wall, why do you not get angry at the wall and blame the wall? Why do we call trees inanimate? Anyone that hurts you is like a tree! If a cow treads on your foot, do you complain about it? So it is the same when people clash with you. Why does the *Gnani Purush* forgive everyone? It is because he knows that people are like the trees; some do not have the understanding. Those who *do* understand, do not need to be told anything; they immediately do *pratikraman*.

You should never see any faults in the other person because when you do, you ruin your worldly life. You have to keep seeing your own faults. You have to understand and accept that everything you encounter in this life is the effect of your own past actions and therefore, no more needs to be said.

Some families make accusations against each other, "You are like this, you are that," even as they share their meals and life together. This is how accounts of revenge are created and this is what perpetuates the worldly life. That is why I tell you to settle all claims with equanimity; when you do, you stop all vengeance.

Worldly Happiness You Indulge In Entraps You Even Deeper

What sweetness is there in this world? Is there any worldly sweetness that lasts? If you eat too much, you will get indigestion and if you eat too little, it will leave you craving more. Happiness should be such that it never makes you uneasy. Behold the bliss Dada experiences, eternal bliss!

People get married to be happy, but on the contrary, they feel even more suffocation after doing so. People get married with the expectation of finding a companion who can be their security blanket or safety net, do they not? There is attraction towards the worldly life, but once you enter it, you find it suffocating, but then you cannot get out. There is a saying:

"The one who eats the wooden *ladoo* regrets doing so, but so does the one who does not eat it."

People get married and then they regret doing so. Regret however, brings experiential knowledge. Is it not necessary to learn through experience? Is it possible to attain detachment (*vairagya*) towards the worldly life by merely reading books? Detachment is acquired only through regret.

Choosing a Life Partner

There was a girl who did not want to get married so her parents brought her to me, and I explained to her, "In life one has no choice but get married and thereafter one has no choice but regret getting married!" I told her that it would be better for her to leave aside all her crying and protests, and just get married. I told her that no matter what kind of a man she married, she would have a husband. Having a husband will stop people from pointing a finger at her. I explained to her the science of how girls should decide on a husband. She understood and got married. She did not find her husband attractive, but married him nevertheless because that is what I told her to do. She acquired *Gnan* before getting married and she did not cross or question a single word I told her. She is very happy now.

Boys are very critical when it comes to choosing a bride.

"She's too tall." "She's too short." "She's too fat." "She's too thin." "She's too dark." You fool! Is she a water buffalo or something? You should explain to your son the method for choosing a bride: go and see the girl and if your eyes are attracted, then that is the sign and the cue to get married and if there is no attraction, then he may say no.

Insult & Vengeance

In arranged marriages, when young men go to choose a bride, they scrutinize the girls and tell them, "Turn around, turn this way, turn that way. Stand this way." One boy was doing this, so I told him, "Your mother was a daughter-in-law once too. What kind of a man are you?" How insulting is it to the woman!" Today there is an overabundance of girls and that is why girls are being insulted so. In the times gone by, these very fools were the subject of ridicule themselves and now they are getting even. In their past lives, five hundred or so of these foolish princes would present themselves in a line one after another at a king's court hoping to be the chosen one for the princess's betrothal. As the princess would walk by with a garland for her potential groom, these fools stood begging with their necks extended forward, each assuming he would be the one! As the princess walked past them, each fool felt so insulted, that he would not bleed even if he got cut. What an unbearable insult! And that too for the sake of simply getting married! It is better to remain a bachelor.

Nowadays, even girls scrutinize the boys and make them turn this way and that way, saying, "Let me see how you look!" Just imagine! You are the one who discovered this system of scrutiny and now you are the victim of it. Just look at your predicament! Instead, is it not better to have no such systems? You dug the hole and now you have to lie in it!

It is only in the past five thousand years or so that men

go out in search of a bride. In the times before, the father of the bride would host a *svayamvar* (gathering of eligible men invited to present themselves at the bride-to-be's house). The *svayamvar* would be attended by a hundred or so fools out of whom the bride would choose one. If this is the process one has to undergo in order to get married, then it is better not to marry. All the fools would line up and the bride would come down with a garland. All the fools would stand there with thousands of expectations and extended necks! This is how the women chose their husbands. Instead, it would be better not to be born at all? Today these fools insult the girls and take their revenge.

Commonsense Will Bring About a Solution

I am not telling everyone to seek liberation, but I *am* telling everyone to learn the art of living. Learn some commonsense from others. Big, wealthy businessmen tell me they already have commonsense. I told one, "If you had commonsense, you would not be in the predicament you are in. You are a dunce!" He then asked me what I meant by 'commonsense'? I replied, "Commonsense is knowledge that is applicable everywhere, both theoretically and practically." No matter how old and rusty a padlock may be, the moment you turn the key, it will open immediately; that is commonsense. However, you cannot open your locks and so you fight and break your locks with a huge hammer.

Do you have differences of opinions? What does it mean to have differences of opinions? If you do not know how to open the lock, from where will you obtain the commonsense to do so? If you do not have 360° worth of commonsense, you should at least have 30–50° worth of commonsense! At least keep this much in your awareness. If you grasp one good thought or idea and hang on to it, it will make you more aware, which in turn, will plant the seeds for more good thoughts and then the process of positive thinking will start. Instead, the wealthy businessmen are only consumed with thoughts of making money and so I tell them, "*Sheth* you are running after money but your household is falling apart, your wife and your children are running around all day." The *sheth* (businessman) then asked me, "So what should I do?" I told him he has to understand how to live life. Do not make money your only pursuit in life. Take care of the dirt in all corners of your home. Do not clean just one corner. Take care of your health or else you will have a heart attack. You have to take care of your money, your health, your children and your wife. You have to clean all the corners of your house. What happens when you tend to just one corner? How can you live your life the way you do right now?

A man with commonsense will not allow any conflict to take place in his home. How can you acquire commonsense? When you sit with the *Gnani* and remain at his feet, and attain *Gnan* from him, you will acquire commonsense. A person with commonsense will not let any conflicts and quarrels occur within or outside his home. How many such households are there in Bombay? How can there be any commonsense where there are conflicts?

If you and your wife start fighting about whether it is daytime or nighttime, where will it all lead to, and when will it come to an end? Instead, you can tell her quietly, "I ask that you to please go and check for yourself, that it is night." If she still insists it is daytime, then you can say, "Yes, you are correct. I made a mistake." Only then will you make any progress. Otherwise, you will never resolve anything. Everyone, including the wife is a passerby.

Even the Body Betrays You In the End

All of your relationships are relative; there is no real

relationship anywhere. Even your body is relative. This body too, is a betrayal. How many relationships this body, this betrayer, have? You take care of this body everyday, you bathe it, you groom it and when you get a stomachache, even if you tell it not to ache, it will. When your tooth starts to hurt, it will make you cry. You brush them everyday for so many years and still they let you down. Everything is a betrayal.

Having been born as a human in the land of India and into a family with high moral and cultural values (all right conditions towards spiritual progress) you should secure your path towards your salvation otherwise you are doomed! Otherwise it will all be futile and go down the drain.

Multiple Solutions for the Husband

It is fine if people do not want liberation, but everyone needs commonsense. People have conflict in their homes due to a lack of commonsense. Not everyone dabbles in the black market do they? Nevertheless, people are still so unhappy. In a home of just three people, there will be countless disagreements and differences of opinions. What happiness can there be in this? Then people live in their own stubborn and insensitive ways. Of what use is life if you do not have any self-respect? A judge comes home after imposing a seven-year jail sentence and yet at home his conflict with his wife remains pending for fifteen days. He does not speak with his wife. If you ask the judge, "Sir why do you not speak with your wife?" he will say, "My wife is really bad, she is totally uncultured." And if you tell his wife, "Your husband is a very good man," she will say, "Do not mention his name to me, he is rotten." Now when you hear such things, can you not figure out that this whole world is empty and without substance? There is no correctness in it.

If the wife buys expensive vegetables, the foolish

husband will pounce on her, "How can you buy such expensive vegetables?" She will accuse him of attacking her and will retaliate with double the force. How can anyone resolve such problems? If your wife buys expensive vegetables, you should say, "Well done! I am very fortunate because a miser like me would never be able to enjoy such expensive vegetables."

I was invited to stay over at someone's house one day. I observed resentment in his wife as she shoved a cup of tea in front of him. I understood immediately that the two must have had a disagreement. I called his wife over and asked her why she was sulking. She said, "It's nothing like that." I told her, "I know what's bothering you. Why are you hiding things from me? When you shoved the teacup in front of him, even your husband understood. Let go of this deceit (kapat) if you want to be happy."

Men are naive and they tend to forgive easily, while women on the other hand, hold on to the events; words their husbands said to them will remain fresh in their minds forty years later. Therefore, you must be cautious when you interact with women. Exercise caution when you want some work done through them. Women will get their work done through you, but you men do not know how to do the same with them.

If your wife wants to buy a sari worth one hundred and fifty rupees, you should give her extra twenty-five rupees. She will be happy for six more months. You have to understand life as it is. You men do not know how to live life and yet you go in search of a wife. You become a husband without qualifications. You must have the certificate for becoming a husband before you earn the right to become a father. Here you men become fathers without qualifications and on top of that, you become grandfathers! When will you wind up everything (the worldly life) and go to moksha? You have to understand.

In the Relative World, Keep Mending

These are all relative relationships; if they were real, then it would be worth your while insisting that you won't rest until your wife changes or improves, but that is not the case. Relative means is when the husband and wife fight with each other for one hour, and then start thinking about a divorce, causing this seed to grow into a big tree. If you have a need for a wife, then even if she keeps tearing away at the relationship, you will have to keep mending it. Only then will this relative relationship last, otherwise it will break. Your relationship with your father is relative also. People believe their relationships with their fathers to be real; they become obstinate about trying to improve him. Let go you fools! He will die before he improves; instead why not just take care of the poor man so he will not bind revenge with you before he dies. Why not let him die peacefully? His stubbornness is his own responsibility. He will have to bear the weight of his horns. Some people have horns twenty feet long but you should not carry the weight, should you?

You have to fulfill your obligations, but you do not have to become uncompromising and adamant in the process. Bring about a quick solution. However, if the other person keeps fighting with you, you can tell him, "I have always been dumb. I do not know what to do." Detach yourself from people in anyway that you can and do not worry about him or her taking control and dominating you. What can anyone do to you? No one has the power to do so. People are dictated by their own karmas, so no matter what, live each day without any conflict and worry about tomorrow when it comes. And, if there is a conflict the next day, do the best you can to bring about a resolution. This is how you should pass your days.

Futility in Trying To Improve Others

If you adjust to the other person in every matter, your life will become very smooth. What are you going to take with you when you die? And if someone tells you to straighten your wife out, and you try to do that, you will become 'twisted' in the process. Whatever your wife may be like, accept the situation a being correct. If your relationship with her were eternal, then it would be a different matter, but she is your wife for this life only. You both will die at different times and you both have different karmas. There is nothing to give or take here. Who knows whose home she will go to after this life? You may end up improving her, but she will end up as someone else's wife.

Questioner : If I bind karma with her, surely we will get together in our next life.

Dadashri : Yes, you may get together, but in some other way. She may come to your house to visit as someone else's wife. There are principles to the laws of karma, are there not? And here, there is no guarantee. Some people with a lot of punya may end up spending several lifetimes together. You know that Lord Neminath and Rajul were together for nine life times; and it would be a different matter if that were the case with you. But here, you do not have a clue about your next life. People separate and go their own way just in this life, do they not? They call it divorce, do they not? Just in this life, some may have two or three husbands.

The Way to Improve Other in This Era

You should not try to improve her and neither should she try to improve you. Whatever you have is gold. No one's *prakruti* ever improves; a dog's tail will always remain crooked so you must exercise caution. Regardless of your wife's personality, accept her as she is and adjust everywhere.

If an occasion for reprimanding arises but you do not say anything, then she will improve. A person, who does not lose his temper or get angry, has tremendous influence. I never get angry with anyone or tell off anyone. Yet people are in awe and have reverence for me.

Questioner : So then, will she improve Dada?

Dadashri : This verily has always been the way to improve others. In this *Kaliyug*, people find it hard to follow this. There is no other alternative.

Questioner : But that is very difficult.

Dadashri : No, it is not difficult. It is the easiest way. A cow has to bear the weight of its own horns.

Questioner : But she will also attack us with her horns, will she not?

Dadashri : Sometimes you may get hurt. If there is likelihood of getting hurt by her horns, then you can move out of the way. In the same way, you should move away when it comes to your wife too. Where do your problems lie? It is in your belief: 'I married her and she is my wife.' Look, there is no such thing as 'wife' and 'husband'. Since there is no husband to begin with, how can there be a wife? These are all acts of ignorance. Where is the trace of *Arya* culture nowadays?

Improve Your Self Only

Questioner : If in all situations I were to accept that I am the one with mistakes, then will doing so improve my wife?

Dadashri : You have to improve yourself if you want to improve others. No one can be improved. Those who try to improve others are all egotistic. If you improve yourself, the other person will improve without fail. I have seen men who have set out to improve others and yet their own wives and mothers have no respect for them. What kind of men are these? First, improve yourself. It is wrong egoism to say or believe you can improve others. When you yourself have no worth, what are you going to do for others? It is necessary for you to become wise first. Lord Mahavir only expended energies in trying to become 'Mahavir' (The Great One) and that is only why millions feel his presence even today. Even now, after twenty-five hundred years, that impression is still strong. I do not try to improve anyone.

Everyone Is a Top

What right do you have to improve others? What right do you have to improve one that has a soul? If this cloth gets dirty, you have the right to clean it, because there will be no reaction from it. Where there is a soul, there will be reactions. What are you going to improve there? When your own *prakruti* does not improve, how are you going to improve someone else's *prakruti*? You yourself are a top (spinning toy) and in the same token, so is everyone else; everyone is under the control of his own *prakruti* because he has not become a *Purush* (Self-realized) yet. Only after one becomes a *Purush* can real effort (*purushartha*) begin. Here, in the world, no one has seen real effort at all.

Your Worldly Life Solved by Adjusting

Questioner : Surely, adjustments cannot just be one-sided if we are to live and continue our worldly interactions in this world.

Dadashri : Proper worldly interactions are ones in which you adjust so that even your neighbors will say, "Every household has conflicts but not this one." It is then that your interactions are considered ideal. You have to cultivate your inner energies in situations where you cannot get along with a person; your strength is already evident in situations where you get along with other people. Inability to get along is a weakness. Why do I get along with everyone? Your energies will grow in proportion with the amount of adjustments you make; your weakness will break by that much. Real understanding will set in when all other worldly understanding is locked out.

The *Gnani* will adjust even with a person who is being awkward. If you observe the *Gnani* and conduct yourself accordingly, you will learn how to adjust everywhere. The science behind this tells you to become *vitarag*, free from attachment and abhorrence. You take a beating because you have subtle attachment within. People who reject and renounce without consideration of the complete situation at hand are considered as being awkward. If there is a need on your part, then you must appease the other person even when he is being awkward. If while you are at the railway station, you need a porter, you will somehow have to appease the porter even if it means giving him a few extra rupees; otherwise you will have to carry your luggage yourself.

Do not see laws; please settle. Where is the time to tell people how to do things? The other person may make hundreds of mistakes, but just tell yourself that the mistake is your own and move on. Is there any point in looking at the law in this day and age? Everything has come to a head here, and very difficult times are coming ahead. Everywhere you look, people are running around, from one place to another. People have become trapped; at home, the wife and children complain, at work the boss complains, and when traveling by train, we get pushed around in the crowd; there is no peace anywhere. Surely, we need some peace. If someone fights with you, you should sympathize with him and try to understand how agitated he has been to become so angry. To become agitated is to become weak.

Questioner : Often I have to adjust with two people at a time over just one issue. How can I deal with situations like that?

Dadashri : You'll be able to do so with both of them. You can even do that with seven people at a time. If one of them asks, "What about me, what will you do for me?" you can tell him, "Yes I will do as you ask." You can say the same to yet another person. Nothing is going to work outside of what is *vyavasthit*, so avoid conflict under any circumstance.

It is because you label everything as 'good' or 'bad', that you are harassed so. Make both the good and the bad equal. If you call this good, the other becomes bad and it will bother you. But, if you mix the two together, you will not be affected. 'Adjust everywhere', is a principle that I have discovered. Adjust with the one who is telling the truth and also with the one who is not. If someone tells me that I have no sense, I would tell him that I never had any to begin with. I would then ask, "Why have you come looking for it now? *You* just discovered this today, but *I* have always known this.' If you say this, there will be no conflict. He will not come to you again looking for sense. If you do not do this, when will you ever reach your home, liberation?

I am showing you this simple, straightforward solution. It is not everyday that you get into an argument is it? It only happens when your past karmas come into fruition, and when that happens, you only need to adjust as much as the situation requires. If you quarrel at home with your wife, then after the quarrel take her out to a restaurant and make her happy. There should be no scope for harboring grudges.

Adjustment is justice. Any form of insistence is not justice. I never insist on anything. We have a saying, "Use whatever water you have to in order to cook the beans.

Ultimately you may even have to use the water from the gutter!"
If you do not adjust and give in to a bandit who is holding you
at knifepoint, he will hurt you. Therefore, you must make a
decision, then adjust with him and get it over with. Ask him,
"What is your wish? We are on our way to a pilgrimage." Do
you fight with the sewer plant of Bandra when it smells? In the
same way, when people smell, do you go to them to complain?
Everything that smells is like a sewer, and everything that has a
nice aroma is like a garden. Everything that comes to you with
a smell, pleasant or unpleasant, is reminding you to remain
vitarag (detached) with it.

If you do not adjust everywhere, you will go mad.
Ongoing harassment and aggravation with the other person will
make you mad. If you keep harassing this dog, he will respect
you a few times, but if you overdo it, he will bite you. The dog
will come to realize, 'This man is no good. He harasses me
everyday. He has no shame.' This is worth understanding. Do
not argue; just adjust everywhere.

The Worldly Confusion Will Become an Obstacle

First, you have to understand worldly interactions; people
suffer a lot because they do not have this understanding.

Questioner : Dada, your spiritual talks are unparalleled,
but so are your talks of interactions of worldly life.

Dadashri : It's like this: no one has attained *moksha*
without understanding the ultimate facts about the worldly life.
It does not matter how priceless the spiritual knowledge is, but
without understanding the worldly life, no one has attained
moksha, because the worldly life has to set you free. What
would you do if it does not set you free? You are a pure soul,
but the worldly life has to set you free, does it not? You keep
entangling your worldly life and making it more complex. Why

do not you bring about a solution quickly?

If you send this man to get some ice cream, he may come back empty-handed. If you ask him why, he will tell you that on the way there he came across a donkey, which is a sign of bad luck, and that is why he came back empty-handed. Now since this man has acquired incorrect knowledge, should we not get rid of it? We should explain to him that God resides in the donkey as well, so there is no such thing as bad luck and that his contempt towards the donkey, reaches the God within and as a consequence, he will incur a tremendous karmic liability. Caution him not to make the same mistake again. People cannot adjust because of incorrect knowledge.

Counter-pulley

You should not voice your opinion first; first ask what the other person thinks. If the other person insists on his viewpoint, I let go of mine. I only consider one thing, that I hurt no one. You should take the other person's viewpoint into consideration, and not try to force your opinion upon them. I have taken everyone's opinion, and only then have I become a *Gnani*. If I ever try to impose my viewpoint on anyone, I would become weak. No one should be hurt because of your opinion. Your revolutions may be at eighteen hundred per minute and the other person's maybe at eight hundred, so if you impose your opinion on the other person, his engine will breakdown and the gears will need to be repaired.

Questioner : What do you mean by 'revolutions'?

Dadashri : It is the speed at which thoughts occur. Everyone has different revolutions. If something happens, the mind will show you many things within just one minute, it shows you many different aspects at a time. All these powerful presidents have eight hundred revolutions, mine are at five thousand. Lord Mahavir's were a hundred thousand!

Why do people have differences of opinions? If your wife's revolutions are at a hundred and yours are at five hundred, there will be conflict if you do not know how to apply a counter-pulley. Many times even the engine breaks down. Do you understand what I mean by revolutions? When you talk to a laborer, your point will not reach him. His revolutions are at fifty, yours are at five hundred and someone else may be a thousand and another person may have twelve hundred. The revolutions are dependent upon an individual's development. You will only get your point across to the other person if you employ a counter-pulley and decrease your revolutions. I use a counter-pulley with everyone. It is not just a matter of getting rid of the ego; I also have to use a counter-pulley with everyone. That is why I never have any differences of opinions with anyone. I am able to understand the person I am dealing with and his limited revolutions, and therefore I use a counter-pulley. I also get along very well with children because I will set a counter-pulley of forty revolutions with them so that they are able to grasp what I am saying, otherwise the machine will break down.

Questioner : Should we speak only after coming down to the level of the other person?

Dadashri : Yes, you should only talk after you come down to their level. Even as I talk to you, my revolutions go all over the place. If you do not know how to use a counter-pulley, what fault is it of the one with fewer revolutions? It is your own fault for not knowing how to use a counter-pulley.

Words Lead To Havoc

Questioner : I cannot take adjustment because I am afraid of my husband and I am afraid of the future; during such instances, I forget your aphorism, 'Who are we to improve others?' and I end up giving advice.

Dadashri : If you apply the *agna* of *vyavasthit*, then there will be no problems. If you do, you will not have any questions. When your husband comes home, get his dinner ready and call him down to eat, do not try to change his *prakruti*. His *prakruti* you were aware of when you chose him to be your husband, has to be observed till the end. Did you not know what his *prakruti* was like from the very beginning? You should have left him from the beginning, why did you allow yourself to be ruined more?

There is no benefit to be gained in your worldly life through nagging; you will only incur a loss. To nag is to quarrel. That is why God has called it a *'kashaya'*.

As problems increase between the two of you, you will start to fall apart. Once the problem is solved, you will not separate. There is sorrow in separation, and besides everyone has problems, you two are not an exception. Problems are inevitable in every marriage.

Quarrels will continue because of past karmas and as they come into effect, but at least stop your negative talking. Keep your personal problems to yourself; do not discuss them within or outside your home.

The Distinct Separation

Questioner : Our *prakrutis* may not improve but at least our worldly interactions (*vyavahar*) should.

Dadashri : People do not know how to conduct their *vyavahar* (worldly interactions) at all. If they had the knowledge, for even half an hour, it would be plenty. No one has understood worldly interactions. What is the definition of 'worldly interactions'? Superficial. The real definition of worldly interactions is that it is not real. It is only superficial! People have believed it to be real. The reality of this worldly life is relative; it is not real. Money, whether it is real or unreal, will be of no use over there on the path of liberation, so let go of your stubbornness and get your work done. Worldly life means receiving what you had given in the past life. If someone were to say, "Chandubhai has no sense," then you should understand that you are getting back what you gave previously. If you understand this, only then it is called *'vyavahar'*, but as such no body knows how to conduct their worldly life. The one whose relative is relative and his real is real, the one established in the knowledge of the Self, is indeed superficial in worldly interactions.

Quarreling Will Stop If You Say It the Right Way (*Samyak*)

Questioner : If someone deliberately throws away something useful, how should we adjust?

Dadashri : In this case, you are talking about some kind of object, but even if for example, he were to drop your little toddler, you have to observe that too. When your husband drops your son, you have to just observe. What else can you do, are you going to throw the husband away also? You'll have to seek medical care for the baby, but do you want to put your husband in the hospital also? And when he has the opportunity to do so, will he not beat you? Do you want triple the medical bills?

Questioner : So should I not say anything at all?

Dadashri : You can, but you have to use the right words with the right tone. Otherwise, what is the point of barking like a dog? So whatever you say must be said properly.

Questioner : What do you mean by 'properly'?

Dadashri : If you exclaim, "Oh ho ho! Why did you drop the baby? What was the reason?" He will reply, "Would

I do it on purpose? He slipped out of my arms and that is why he fell."

Questioner : But he is telling a lie, is he not?

Dadashri : Whether he tells a lie or not is not your concern. Whether he tells the truth or tells lies, it is of his own freewill; he is not dependent upon you. He will do as he pleases. If he wants to tell a lie, or do away with you, that is in his control. If he were to poison your water at night, you will die for sure! Therefore, you need not concern yourself with what is not under your control. If you know how to speak properly, you should say, "Dear what did you gain by doing that?" and maybe then he will admit his mistake. You do not know how to speak properly; you just lash out and so he will retaliate with double the force.

Questioner : If I do not know how to speak to him properly, what should I do? Should I remain silent?

Dadashri : Remain silent and observe. What do you do when you see little children being abused in a movie? Everyone has the right to say something, but only if it is not going to result in conflict. It is foolishness to speak in a manner which results in conflict.

Pratikraman for Words That Hurt

Questioner : If someone is doing something wrong, what should we do if it hurts him if we caution him? How do we resolve that situation?

Dadashri :, You have to caution them from the worldly perspective, but because this happens through the ego, you have to do *pratikraman*.

Questioner : If I do not caution him, will he not end up dominating me?

Dadashri : You have to caution him, but you must know how to speak. Because you do not know how to speak, you end up doing it through your ego. It is simply that you do not know how to interact, that you end up doing so through your ego. And that is why you must do *pratikraman* afterwards. When you try to caution or correct the other person, he is bound to feel hurt, but if you keep doing pratikraman for it, several months down the road, the speech that will emanate from you will be appealing to the other person. Currently you will need 'tested' speech. You do not have the right to utter 'untested speech'. If you do *pratikraman* in this manner, then no matter what, everything will work out.

Not On Talking Terms Increases Conflict

Questioner : Is it possible to dissipate conflict by not speaking to the other person?

Dadashri : No, it is not possible. You should speak to the other person if you encounter them. You should ask how he is doing. If the other person reacts with hostility, you should quietly try to resolve the situation with equanimity. You will have to resolve the situation, sooner or later. Just because you do not speak to the other person, does not mean that the problem has been resolved. It is because the problem has not been resolved that people end up not speaking to each other. Not speaking to the other person means there is a burden of the unresolved conflict. You should approach the other person and say, "Tell me if I have done something wrong. I make a lot of mistakes. You are a very intelligent person, you are learned and you do not make many mistakes. I however, am not as learned and so I make a lot of mistakes." If you say this to other person, he will be appeased.

Questioner : What if he does not calm down even after I say this?

Dadashri : What can you do if he does not calm down? Once you say this to him, you are free, what other solution is there? He will calm down someday. You cannot soften the other person by telling him off. He may appear to have calmed down but from within he makes a mental note of it and will throw it in your face when you least expect it. So understand that his world lives on vengeance. The fact is that people will continue to harbor vengeance; they retain atoms of revenge within so you must try to resolve the situation completely.

Adjust According to Their *Prakruti*

Questioner : What should I do if I try to break the silence by asking for forgiveness from the other person but instead, he reacts even more negatively?

Dadashri : Then you should not say anything to him. If he has the misconception of, 'The one who gives in is a weakling,' then you should stay away from him. Then, whatever happens is correct. However, resolve everything with those who are straightforward and easy to deal with. Can you not tell who in your household is easy to get along with and who is difficult?

Questioner : If the other person is not straightforward, should we sever the relationship with him?

Dadashri : Do not sever it. Worldly interactions are not such that they will break by you breaking them. You should just remain silent and then one day he or she will get angry and bring about a resolution. If you remain quiet, then one day she will get angry and ask you, "You do not say anything anymore. You have not said anything for so many days." When she gets angry, you will resolve things. What else can you do? There are so many different types of iron; I can understand them all. Certain types of iron become malleable when heated while others require being left in the kiln and then with a few strokes of a hammer you can beat the metal into shape. There are so many different kinds of irons; the soul within is the pure soul; it is *paramatma* (the Supreme Soul) and iron is the iron. These are all elements.

Declare Your Faults Openly

Questioner : I am not attentive towards certain matters in the home. People at home keep telling me to be more attentive and alert, but I am unable to do so. What should I do?

Dadashri : Nothing. If people in the house tell you to pay attention, then you should say, "Yes, I will," and you should decide to do so. Despite doing this, if something goes wrong, then you should tell them you are not able to maintain your attention. You will have to bring about a resolution will you not? If someone tells me to pay attention to something, I will, but if despite doing so, I slip up, I will tell them that I was not able to do it.

It is like this, if you are able to forget the fact that you are older, then you will be able to accomplish your task. If you become like a child, you will be able to resolve matters with equanimity very nicely. I am like a child, and that is why I tell it like it is. I may say one thing or another. What use is there in exercising seniority?

Those who are faced with trials and tribulations are blessed, so deal with your problems and do not become stubborn. You should expose your fault by stating so, directly and openly. And if the other person is blaming you, then you should be happy and tell them you are glad that they discovered your mistake.

Red Flag-Green Flag

There must be some mistake on your part, which is why

the other person is pointing it out, so destroy your mistakes. No one is able to harass anyone in this world; that is how independent the whole world is. And whatever trials and tribulations you have to face are because of your own past misdeeds, your own karmas. Destroy your mistakes and you will not have to deal with any more accounts.

If someone raises a red flag at you, you must understand that you are at fault somewhere, so ask the other person why he is raising the red flag. When he tells you your mistake, you should ask for his forgiveness and ask him if he would wave a green flag at you from now on and he will say yes.

No one holds a red flag in front of me. I do not proceed until I see green flags from everyone. If I am leaving to go elsewhere and someone raises a red flag at me, I will stop and ask him why he has objections. He may say, "The other day you said you were not going to leave until next week, so how come you are leaving early?" I would clear the air with him and explain to him that certain matters have come up and therefore, I have no choice but to leave. He would then willingly say, "Then please go. I have no objection."

People wave red flags at you because of your mistakes, but if you take the trouble to clear up the air, then no one will object. Instead, when people raise a red flag, you start ranting and raving, "You idiot! Why are you behaving this way? What is your problem?" This is how you attack them. You do not realize that you are creating a whole, new problem. When someone waves a red flag at you, understand that something is wrong. Otherwise, no one would do so.

How Can You Afford To Have Altercations Everyday?

Dadashri : Do you have quarrels in your home?

Questioner : Yes.

Dadashri : Are your quarrels mild or do you truly fight with each other?

Questioner : Sometimes we truly fight, but we forget about it the next day.

Dadashri : What else would you do if not forget? It is only when you forget that you quarrel again. Who would quarrel again if he did not forget? People live in big bungalows and even though there are only five people in it, they fight. Nature gives them food and shelter yet even then people quarrel. People are only good at fighting and quarreling.

Quarrels only arise among underdeveloped people. It is because they do not know how to arrive at the totality of the situation that they fight.

There are as many religions as there are people, but how is one to build a temple of his own religion? Nevertheless, everyone's *dharma* is different. When people sit to do *samayik* (meditative introspection), everyone's *samayik* is different. Alas! Some people sit in the back and throw tiny pebbles at the ones doing *samayik*! Such people too, will do their own *samayik*! There is absolutely no religion left in this and neither any meaning. If there were any trace of religion left, there would be no quarrels in the homes and if any quarrels were to take place, there would be only one or so a month. The dark phase of the moon only comes once a month does it not?

Questioner : Yes.

Dadashri : Here people have the dark phase all thirty days of the month! What do people get when they quarrel?

Questioner : There is only loss.

Dadashri : No one would invest in a business that is unprofitable. No one is telling them to do so either. Surely, they must gain something from it.

Questioner : Maybe they get enjoyment from quarreling.

Dadashri : Peace does not prevail because of the current time cycle, so the one burning, only finds peace when he burns others. He does not like it if someone is happy, he only finds peace when he lights the wick before he leaves. This is the nature of the world today. Even the animals are courteous, they do not quarrel. Even the dogs stick together amongst their own group and fight united against other dogs, whereas these foolish people fight amongst each other! People have no courtesy nowadays.

Become Quarrel-proof

Questioner : I have no desire to quarrel under any circumstances, but what should I do if people in the household start a quarrel?

Dadashri : You should become quarrel-proof, only then will you be able to live in this worldly life. I will make you quarrel-proof. Your nature should become such that even people looking for a quarrel, will get tired. You should become such that absolutely no one in the world can depress you. If you become quarrel-proof then there is no problem. Even if people want to quarrel with you or shout abuses at you, there will be no problems. And despite doing this, you cannot be considered thick-skinned, on the contrary your spiritual awareness will increase many fold.

Seeds of Revenge: Trees of Quarrels

Whatever quarrels you had committed in your past life had created revenge, and that revenge manifests in the form of a quarrel today. The seeds of revenge are sown the moment quarreling takes place, and these seeds will then grow in the next life.

Questioner : So how can we distance ourselves from those seeds?

Dadashri : As you gradually begin to settle matters with equanimity, you will keep those seeds at bay. If the seed was very heavy to begin with, it will take some time and you have to be patient. No one can take anything away from you. As long as you have clothes to wear and two meals a day, what more do you need?

Even if they lock you up in your room before they leave, all you have to concern yourself with is whether you get two meals a day or not. There is no problem if they lock you up in your room. You should just go to sleep. You had created such karma of revenge in your past life, which is why in this life they lock you up before they leave. It is nothing but revenge, bound in a state of ignorance. If there is any kind of understanding or rationale to it, we can try to solve the problem. However, when you cannot make any sense of it, how are you to resolve the matter? Therefore, you must let go in such matters.

Gnan is Freedom from All Conflicts

Now you have to break free from all revenge, so come to me and take knowledge of self-realization, then you will be set free. You have to become free from all revenge in this very life and I will show you the way. Why do people seek death when they are fed up with life? It is because they do cannot deal with this kind of stress. Surely, you will have to understand everything. How long can you continue living under so much pressure? The life of human beings today has become like that of insects, they are in perpetual torment. Why should there be any torment after one is born as a human? Is such a state becoming for the one who is the lord of the fourteen universes?

The whole world is in a state of torment and if there is no torment, then there prevails a state of illusion. The world is not outside the parameters of these two states. When you become the enlightened Self, you are free from all torments and illusion.

Gnan Tested In Adversity

Questioner : If someone is playing a big drum, why does it upset an irritable person so much?

Dadashri : It is because he does not like it. If a person is playing the drum, you have to say, "You play the drum very well." By saying this, you will not be affected internally. Once you have the opinion of, 'This is annoying,' then everything from within becomes ruined. So you have to make a positive comment in a 'dramatic' (make believe) manner.

Because of this *Gnan* you will be able to make all kinds of payments of karmic debts. This *Gnan* is extremely beneficial in difficult circumstances. You will be tested and will pass. Even if you practice *Gnan* everyday, it will not be as well-tested as when you face difficult circumstances.

The Dance Of Past Karmas

It would be a different matter if after quarreling with your wife; you would have nothing to do with her. However, you have no choice, you will have to get along with her so all the quarreling is useless and wrong. I am always aware of the fact that after an hour or two, we will have to speak with each other and therefore I do not harp on anything. It is a different matter if your opinion will never need to be changed and if you were never to sit with your wife again, then your quarreling is correct. But here, you have to sit and dine with her the very next day, so of what use is all the drama between the two of you? Will you not have to think about this? Instead, what people do is cook the seeds before they sow them and so all their effort is in vain. Whenever you are quarreling, you must maintain awareness that it is your past karma that makes you dance. Therefore, you must settle all this 'dancing' through your *Gnan*.

Questioner : But Dada surely both the quarreling parties must remember this.

Dadashri : No, here each has to mind his or her own business. If you improve, only then will the other person improve. Just think a little, when after awhile you both have to be together, why then should you quarrel? Once you enter into a marriage, why should there be any quarreling? You forget incidents that took place yesterday, whereas for me, everything remains present in my *Gnan*. Mind you, this thinking is a virtuous and is helpful for even those who do not have *Gnan*. It is out of ignorance that people believe their spouse will try to control them. But, if someone were to ask me, I would tell him, "You are a top and so is she, so how is she going to control you? Do you think that the control is in her hands?" Everything is under the control of *vyavasthit*. And even if your wife were to control you, what is she going to do? If you were to give in a little, your poor wife will feel a sense of comfort in her mind that you have come under her control! She will be at peace.

Suspicion Leads to Conflicts

Most of the quarreling today stems from suspicion. Suspicion creates vibrations that ignite into flames, and if one becomes free from suspicion, then these flames will automatically extinguish. If both the husband and wife become suspicious, then how can these flames be extinguished? One of you has no choice but to become suspicion-free. Quarrels between parents ruin the impressions on children's psyche (*sanskar*), so both the parents must work towards settling matters with equanimity. How can you get rid of suspicion? This *gnan* of ours can you make you completely suspicion-free. The soul has infinite powers!!

All Speech Is a Taped Record

If you get hurt because you bumped into a table, you do not consider the table at fault. But, if someone hurts you, you see him or her as the guilty one responsible for the act. When a dog barks at you, but does not hurt you, you put up with it. In the same token, if a person does not harm you but merely barks at you, should you not put up with him also? To bark means to speak. Don't they sometimes make a comment like, "This woman barks a lot!"? Even lawyers bark in the courtrooms, do they not? The judge watches two lawyers bark. Do lawyers not bark without being emotionally involved? Inside the courtroom, they make all kinds of accusations against each other and we feel that the two of them will get into a fight, but outside the courtroom, the two sit and leisurely drink tea together!

Questioner : Is that called 'fighting dramatically'?

Dadashri : No, that is called 'parrot play'. No one other than a *gnani* knows how to act dramatically. Parrot play is where people watching the interaction between the two, feel that they are going to kill each other, but in fact they are merely pecking at each other with their beaks, they peck without hurting each other.

Have I not said that all speech is a recording (tape)? If a recording keeps saying, 'Mani has no sense...Mani has no sense,' then you too should sing along with the record, 'Mani has no sense!'

Pratikraman Reveals the Knot of Attachment

You should do *pratikraman* for your husband throughout the day as you do your work. You can clear up six months worth of revenge in just one day. Even if you do half a day's worth of *pratikraman*, you can be sure that you have cleared up at least three months worth of revenge! Did you have any attachment with your husband before you married him? No. So how did you become bound by attachment? As you sat across the groom under the wedding canopy, you thought to yourself and accepted, 'He is my husband, he is a little plump and a little dark.' He too decided and accepted, 'She is my wife.' The knot of attachment that began at that moment has continued to multiply to this day. This film of the past fifteen years will need to be unwound by you by telling yourself, 'He is not mine... he is not mine.' When these knots are undone then the attachment will be gone, but not otherwise. In reality, your opinions began to form from the day of your marriage. This has led to your prejudices of, 'He is like this, he is like that.' Where were these prejudices before? From now on, you should decide, 'Whatever he is like, I accept him. I was the one that chose him,' and besides, is now the time to change your husband?

Traps Are Everywhere, Where is One to Go?

What do you do when there is no solution? You cannot complain or cry about things that have no solutions. This worldly life is mandatory. A person is obligated to carry out his duties even if he does not like the quarrelsome nature of his wife, his brother or his parents; if he is trapped amongst such a crowd, he has no choice but stay. He feels suffocated by this trap, but where can he go? There is a wall all around him and he is trapped within. There is a wall of societal pressure; 'What will people say, if I leave?' There is also a legal wall. If his predicament drives him to commit suicide at Juhu Beach, the policeman will detain him. He may say to the policeman, "Look here Sir, please let me die in peace." The policeman will say, "Sir we cannot let you do that. Suicide is illegal so I will have to arrest you." So, they will not let you die and neither will they let you live; that is called 'worldly life'. Therefore, just try to live peacefully, smoke your cigarette and rest. Such is this worldly life; everything in it is compulsory and mandatory. They will not let you live and neither will they let you die.

So try to adjust any way that you can and pass the time so that your karmic debts are paid off and cleared. You may have a debt of twenty-five years with someone, fifteen years with another, ten years with another and thirty years with someone else; you have no choice but pay off the debt. Whether you like it or not, you have no choice but live in the same room as that person. You sleep on one side and she sleeps on the other and even if you turn your back to each other, your thoughts are of each other. There is no escaping. This indeed is the nature of this world. What is more, it is not only that you do not like her; she too may not like you. There is no happiness in this world.

A thinking person cannot afford to have conflicts that create worldly bondage. A non-discerning person is not even aware of the trap and the bondage in clashing. If you say something derogatory about a deaf man in his presence, he would be unaffected because he simply cannot hear. In the same way, people are deaf on the inside. This is the ignorance, and that is why they put up with all the quarrels and the conflicts. People look for happiness in the worldly life, how can there ever be happiness in it?

Why Protect That Has No Value?

This whole world is hollow and without substance. People bicker and fight inside their homes but when they go out, they wash their faces before they leave! And if you ask them how they are doing, they will reply, "Very well." You fool! There are tears in your eyes and you may have washed your face but your eyes are still all red! Instead, why not just tell people you are unhappy at home. Everyone believes there is happiness in everyone else's home except his or her own. They

do not realize that everyone else is crying also. Everyone
washes their faces before they leave home. You would find out
just how much happiness there is in this world, if people were
to leave their homes without washing their faces. If I come
outside crying, you do the same and he does the same, then you
will realize that this world is nothing but empty. A man buries
his father at a very young age, he cries all the way to the
crematorium, comes home and takes a shower and that is the
end of that! They teach people to take a bath and get clean;
that is the world for you. Everyone washes his or her face
before leaving the home; they all put up a show, they are all
deceivers! Instead, it would be better if they all tell the truth
openly.

Of all our *mahatmas* (self-realized people), there will be
a rare man who will tell me, "Dada, my wife beat me up today!"
From where did this man acquire such candidness? Such
candidness comes because of this *Gnan*. You can tell 'Dada'
everything. Such candidness is the sign of approaching liberation.
How else can there be such candidness? One needs to be
straightforward if he is to acquire liberation. The husband may
get away with telling a lie outside, but at home, he takes a
beating from his wife. Even then, outside he will say, "Oh! That
was our daughter my wife was beating!" You fool! I saw with
my own eyes that it was *you,* she was beating! What is the use
of lying? It is all meaningless. Instead, why not tell the truth?
The soul never takes a beating. You are the Soul and so even
when she gives a beating it is the body that she beats. No one
can insult our soul, because they can only do so if they can see
the soul. How can they insult that which they cannot see? On
the other hand, even buffaloes can hurt the body, can they not?
When this happens, do men not openly declare that the buffalo
hit them? And is the wife not higher than the buffalo? So what?
What reputation are you trying to protect? Did you even have

a reputation to begin with? How many living entities are there in this world? Do any of them have to wear clothing? Those with reputation do not need to clothe themselves. Only those who have no reputation wear clothes and hide behind them, and if their clothes are torn, they quickly stitch them up. Someone may see! You fools! For how many days can you preserve your reputation by patching all the tears? A reputation that needs mending cannot last. Reputation is only to be found where there is an obliging nature, principles, honesty, and kindness.

This is How the Trap Deepens

Man has to marry for his food! He may think to himself, 'I am the bread winner,' but who will do the cooking? The woman knows that although she knows how to cook, she wonders who is going bring home the money. This is how the two get married and organize a company. After that, there will even be children. Once the seed of a squash is planted, will it not naturally give rise to many squashes? A squash will grow at every leaf of the vine. This is the same with humans except that the squash does not say, "These are all my offspring." Only humans claim, "These are my children."

The humans are considered to be unprotected and destitute, because of their dependency on the intellect. No other living entity is dependent upon the intellect and therefore they are all protected and sheltered. Those who have protection can never be unhappy. Only the human species experiences unhappiness. This constitutes misuse of the intellect.

Man runs around in vain chasing illusionary happiness and when his wife turns against him, he realizes that this worldly life is not meant for enjoyment or indulging in. Yet, he forgets this fact again the very next moment! Because of this illusion he takes such a beating, it renders him completely oblivious to the reality.

Man remembers God when his wife is sulking and will not speak with him, but once she starts talking to him, he is ready to put God and everything else aside. What suffocation! Do you think your suffering is going to end this way? Do you think your unhappiness will cease by you spending a few moments with God? Your internal torment is abated for the duration you are with God but otherwise the furnace within continues to burn! The fire is constantly burning, without a moment's relief. Unless and until you acquire the knowledge of your Self, until you have realization of, 'My real nature is pure Soul,' this fire will burn relentlessly. Even when your daughter is getting married, there is suffering within. It is constantly there. What is the meaning of this worldly life? It is nothing but entanglements of suffering. This body also that has taken hold of you is also an entanglement. Can anyone ever have fondness for entanglements? It is a wonder indeed that people have fascination and fondness for the worldly life! There is a difference between the fishing net and the worldly net. An escape from the fishing net is possible if one can cut the net, but there is no escape whatsoever from this worldly net, except upon death.

Be Free From Within

Will you not have to understand the fact that there is no happiness in this worldly life? Your brothers insult you, your wife insults you, and your children insult you! All these are temporary relationships. Do you think they will come with you when you die?

You are the pure Soul and the worldly life is superficial, which means there is no involvement on your part. You have to remain in your 'home department' (real-Self), and the relative self has to remain in the 'foreign department' (non-self). By telling you to remain 'superficial', I mean that you do not become entangled; you should not have the inclination to become entangled or become one with your worldly life and affairs, that is what I call being dramatic or 'play-acting'. All you have to do is merely play your part in this drama of life. So, if, in this drama you incur a loss, you should show unhappiness and smile when you incur a profit. In this worldly drama if you incur a loss, you have to act accordingly and pretend to appear sad and you may even tell people that you incurred a terrible loss, but from within you must keep the separation between what is real and what is relative, and not become emotionally entangled.

Just keep your distance. Have you not heard people say, "I keep my distance with that man,"? You have to live in exactly the same way with this entire world from within. Those who master this, become *Gnani*! Keep your distance even with this body of yours! I always keep my distance with everyone, from the inside. Despite this everyone tells me, "Dada you have so much affection for me." I fulfill all my worldly interactions but by remaining within my domain as the pure Self.

Questioner : What should we do if sometimes there is a major conflict in our home?

Dadashri : A wise man would never get into any conflict, even if he were offered a hundred thousand rupees. But, people fight every moment without any financial reward. Is that not sheer stupidity? Lord Mahavir had to leave his home and walk miles and miles in search of penance in order to dissipate his karma, and this he was able to accomplish amidst barbaric and dangerous people. People today are so fortunate that they find such individuals in their very homes! What tremendous fortune! This is so helpful and beneficial towards dissipating your karma, providing you remain in *Gnan*!

An Hour of Wrongdoing but a Punishment of a Lifetime!

If you were to continuously scold your servant, your

child, or your wife for just one hour, then in your next life they will come to you as your wife or your mother-in-law, and torment you your entire life! Is justice not needed? This is what you have to suffer. If you ever hurt anyone, then you will have to face a lifetime of suffering. If you hurt someone for just one hour, you will have to tolerate a lifetime worth of suffering. Then you will complain and question, 'Why is my wife treating me this way?' and your wife is asking herself, 'Why do I behave this way with my husband?' She too feels unhappy but what can anyone do? I asked one man whether he chose his wife or whether his wife chose him, and he told me he had chosen his wife. So how can you blame the poor wife? Once you bring her home and she turns out to be contrary to your expectations, what can she do? Where is she to go? Many women actually beat their husbands!

Questioner : If a man takes the beating, is he not considered spineless and a weakling?

Dadashri : Accepting a beating is not considered a weakness in a man. His karmic ties are such that his wife has come to him for the sole reason of making him suffer and she has no choice but avenge the karmic tie between them.

The 'Tops' Are Clashing And Bleeding Mentally

You should never consider scolding anyone in your life. Scolding is really a disease. To scold someone is nothing but ego, overt ego and a mad one at that. A person may think to himself, 'Unless I tell him off, he will not shape up.' On the contrary, scolding someone will put a strain on you. Do people enjoy reprimanding others?

At home, you should only give advice if someone asks for it. God has said that giving advice to anyone without being asked is egoism. You may ask your wife where to put the drinking glasses and when she tells you, you should simply put them where she tells you. Some men will make a comment like, "Do you not have any sense where to put them?" The wife will then make a comment like, "So use your own sense and put them away!" Now how can there be an end to such situations? These are nothing but events clashing. These are all tops clashing with each other; they clash when they eat; they clash the moment they wake up. These tops bang into each other and get hurt and they even bleed! The blood that oozes is from their minds. It would be better to bleed physically, that way at least you could dress the wound. But, can anyone dress the wounds of the mind?

Gnani's Words Heal All Wounds

To say anything to anyone in your home is a major disease of the ego. Everyone has brought with them their own karmic accounts! Events are naturally unfolding for each and everyone, you do not have to tell them, 'Do this,' or 'Why do you not do that?' Each one is looking through his eyes; each one is listening through his ears! There is no need to interfere at all. Do not say even a single word to anyone and that is why I am giving you this knowledge of *vyavasthit*. The world is never, even for a moment, outside the laws of *vyavasthit*. Even when it appears not to be *vyavasthit*, it is *vyavasthit*. Therefore, you only need to understand the facts. If sometimes your kite takes a plunge, you simply have to pull on its string. You now have control of the string (this is applicable to the one who has received *Gnan*). But what can a person do if he does not have the control over the string? The control is not in his hands and he is cries out, "My kite is falling, my kite is falling!"

You should cease to say anything to anyone in the home. No one can say a word except a *Gnani*. Why is that? This is because the speech of the *Gnani* is dependent upon the wishes of the other person. The *Gnani* speaks for the benefit of the other person. Why would I have the need to speak? The *Gnani's* speech emanates purely for the purpose of fulfilling the wishes of others. But, when others speak, before they say even a word, there will be so much disruption; so many karmas come to be bound. You should not speak even a word! To utter anything at all, is considered nagging. Speech worthy of being called speech is one that others like to hear, even when that person is reprimanding, people like listening to him. But otherwise, before you utter even a word, they tell you to stop nagging and interfering. Reprimanding can only be beneficial if you do so without any prejudice, but prejudice is inevitable. Prejudice means to make mental notes, 'Yesterday he did such and such and I had to tell him off. That is so typical of him.' According to God the one who reprimands members of the family, is foolish. It is a sign of going to hell when you hurt anyone.

The Fishing Line and the Bait

No other living species, except man exercises his authority as a husband. Nowadays, they file for a divorce! They tell their attorneys, "I will pay you two thousand rupees, if you handle my divorce." The attorney will agree, the foolish man! Why not take a divorce yourself instead of getting one for others?

I will tell you a story of an old lady I knew. As she was preparing for *savarni* (ritual after the death of a loved one where things dear to the departed one, are gathered on a bed, and given to the priest), she said, "Your uncle liked to eat this and he also like to eat this..." She carried on this manner as she made her nephew put things on the *savarni* bed. I told her, "Dear mother, you used to fight with uncle all the time, and sometimes uncle used to beat you too. So why are you doing all this?" She replied, "Nevertheless, I will never be able to find a husband like your uncle.' Such are the value systems in India!

Who is worthy of being called a husband? It is the one who maintains and upholds the social structure of the marital life. Who is worthy of being called a wife? It is the one who maintains and upholds the same. How can you possibly call them husband and wife when they break and tear away at the structure of the marital life? If you get angry with your wife, is it right for you to break this water pot? Some people even break their chinaware and then go out and buy new ones. You foolish people, if you were going to buy them, why break them in the first place? People lose all sense of what is right and wrong when anger blinds them.

Men become husbands, but a true husband is one whose wife will want to look at his face all day long.

Questioner : They do that before marriage.

Dadashri : Really she is casting a fishing line. The fish thinks this person is very kind and will take care of them, but try biting on that line; the hook on the line will trap you. It is all nothing but entrapment!

Sexual Attraction Is Not Love

You can only say you have acquired something worthwhile from those in your home when they feel love towards you and they do not like it when you are away and they look forward to you coming home.

People get married but there is no love. It is only sexual attraction. If there were true love between them, then no matter how much they disagree with each other, their love would not wane. Where there is no true love, it is all simply an attraction. Attraction means excrement! There used to be so much love in the days gone by, that whenever the husband was away, the wife's *chit* was completely absorbed in her husband and no one else would come to mind. Today however, if the husband has been away for two years, she will find a new husband! How can you call this love? This is nothing but excrement! That which flows out is called excrement. In true love, there is giving, not taking.

Love is that which keeps you engrossed and stays on your mind all day long. There are two conclusions in marriage: sometimes it thrives and sometimes it results in destruction. The love that overflows can also ebb. That which overflows is really attraction, so keep your distance from where it overflows. The burning flame of true love is an internal state. Even when the external packing spoils, or decays, the love remains the same. But if the wife burns her hand and asks her husband to help her change the dressing, he will say he cannot bear to look at her hand. The fool! This is the same hand that you were caressing, and now you are repulsed by it? How can you put up with this? Where there is love, there is no repulsion and where there is repulsion, there is no love. Even the worldly love needs to be without great fluctuation. It should be within normality. The *Gnani's* love never increases or decreases; it is unique, and is considered to be the love of the Absolute Soul.

Normality Worthy of Learning

Questioner : What is the definition of 'normality' in this worldly life?

Dadashri : If everyone tells you that you wake up late, should you not understand that you are not within normality? If you wake up in the middle of the night and roam around the house, will people not ask you why you wake up so early? That too is not within normality. Normality is that which is acceptable to everyone around. You need normality even in your eating habits. If you overeat, you will feel sleepy. You should observe the normality in my eating and drinking. There is normality in all my actions, sleeping, waking, etc. If someone puts a little extra dessert on my plate, I will adjust and decrease the intake of other foods accordingly. I am aware 'There is extra dessert on the plate so I will not eat the vegetables.' You do not have to do all this. If you get up late, you have to keep telling your file No. 1, 'Chandulal, you are not able to remain within normality.' You have to keep yourself in check. Tell Chandulal, 'You should wake up early.' Cautioning yourself this way will become beneficial. This is your real effort. By forcing yourself to wake up early, you will ruin your mind.

Dissipation of Human Energy

Questioner : 'The husband is the Lord.' What is wrong in this statement?

Dadashri : If women went around believing husbands of today to be Lords, the husbands will become increasingly mad through their intoxication of 'I am something'.

One husband told his wife, "Put hot coals on your head and cook your bread on it." As it is he has the traits of a monkey so what would happen if you give him alcohol?

A real man is one who has an aura, which commands the respect of thousands of women. Just the mere sight of such a man makes the women tremble. But, the men of today are such that if Salia was holding his wife's hand, he will plead, "Please Salia, let go of her hand. She is my wife. She is my wife." You idiot! Why are you pleading to Salia? What kind of a fool are you? You need to hit him, grab hold of his throat and bite him. Salia is not one to leave your wife alone because of your pleading. Instead, the husband then calls out, "Police, police! Please help me!" You fool, after becoming a husband why are

you calling out to the police? What are you going to do with the
policeman? Are you living or are you dead? If you are going to
depend on the police for help then do not become a husband.

You cannot be a 'half-around' man and be a husband.
You need to be 'all-around'. There are six requirements to be
called a man: 1. He should have the ability to write. 2. He
should be able to cook, so that he is not dependent upon others
for his nourishment. 3. He should be skilled in his ability to
protect. 4. He should have the ability to convince others in
order to get his work done. 5. He should have the art of
survival. 6. He should be a master in the art of stealing or
pilfering. A man unable to carry out these six tasks is not a man.
A true man knows how to adjust with the other person even if
that person is the most devious and debased. To not lose your
mind when dealing with such a person is what really counts, it
is of no use if you become angry and aggravated.

A man who has absolute faith in himself will have
everything, but alas men have lost faith in themselves! Some
men have lost faith even in their wife and have doubts about
whether his wife will remain with him. 'Will she put up with me
for even five years or not?' You fool! You do not have
confidence even in this matter? Once a person loses faith, it is
the end of him. There is tremendous strength in faith, even if that
faith is in the form of ignorance. Once a person worries, 'What
is to become of me?' then he is doomed. In this day and age
people have become confused.

A Bolt with Crooked Threads

Questioner : I try very hard to adjust with my wife, but
I am not able to.

Dadashri : Everything in life is a repayment. When the
threads of a bolt are crooked, how is it possible to fit a bolt

with straight threads into it? You may ask yourself, 'Why is the woman like this?' The woman is really your counter weight. Her awkwardness is in proportion to the degree of your faults. So this is all *vyavasthit*, do I not tell you this?

Questioner : It seems that everyone has come to sort me out and shape me up!

Dadashri : You need to shape up. The world cannot function without people shaping up, can it? If you do not shape up, how will you become a father? Shape up and then you can become a father.

Woman's Divine Energy

That is why women are not at fault, women have the energies of divine beings. There is a soul in women and men, but only the outer packing is different. The differences lie only in the packing. A woman is an effect of a kind; this effect has an effect on the soul within. This effect must not affect you. Women represent energy. Women have done well in high government positions in India. If a woman were to devote herself towards religion and spirituality, she has the power and energy to do salvation for the entire world. She will accomplish her own salvation and has the power do the same for the whole world.

Pratikraman: The Master Key

Questioner : Some men run away from home because they have had enough of their wives. What is all that about?

Dadashri : No, why should men run away? We are the supreme soul, why must we have the need to become a runaway? We have to settle and discharge matters with equanimity.

Questioner : How can we settle with equanimity?

Should we accept in our mind that the severe conflicts we face
are from our previous life?

Dadashri : You cannot discharge your karmas by doing
only that. By 'discharge', we mean that you should make a
connection with the other person and notify the soul within him.
Admit to the soul within that person that you have made many
mistakes. You have to do significant *pratikramans*.

Questioner : If the other person insults me, do I still
have to do his *pratikraman*?

Dadashri : You have to do *pratikraman* only if he
insults you, not if he treats you with respect. If you do
pratikraman, you will not have any feelings of abhorrence
towards him. Furthermore, he will be aware of the positive
vibrations from your *pratikraman*. The first step is that there
are no feelings of abhorrence towards him but the second step
is that the other person becomes aware of this.

Questioner : It really reaches his soul?

Dadashri : Yes, it reaches for sure. The soul then tells
him, 'There has been a call for you.' Our *pratikramans* are for
acts of aggression, not for routine mundane activities.

Questioner : Do we have to do many *pratikramans*?

Dadashri : The faster you want to build your house, the
more workers you have to employ. If you fail to do
pratikraman with people at large, it will do but you have to do
pratikraman of those around you and in your home. For those
in your home, you must have the inner intent that those who are
born, around you, and to you, should some day get on the path
of liberation.

With Adjustments All Conflicts Will Dissolve

The one who learns the art of adjusting is the one who

has turned towards the path of liberation. To have made an adjustment is *Gnan*. The one who has learnt to adjust is considered having won. Whatever you have to suffer, you have no choice but suffer. There is no problem for the one who knows how to adjust and his karmic account will be cleared. Everyone can adjust with people who are easy to get along with, but if you are able to adjust with those who are awkward, difficult, and stubborn, then you have accomplished your work. Adjustment is the main thing. To say yes to everything, is liberation. Even if you give in, nothing is going to happen outside the realms of *vyavasthit*. But, if you say no, or you oppose, then you will have problems.

If both the husband and wife make a decision jointly that they want to adjust with each other, then it is possible for both to achieve their goals. Or, if one of you pulls more, the other should give in more; even then you can resolve matters. A man has pain in his arm but he tells no one, instead he uses his good arm to massage the other one. In this way, if you are able to adjust, you will accomplish your work. Nothing will be achieved through conflicts. Even though you do not like conflicts, you still have them do you not? If the other partner is being adamant and keeps pulling, you should just let go and go to sleep. But, if you both keep pulling, neither of you will be able to sleep and your whole night will be ruined. You take so much care in your worldly transactions, your partnership, your business, and all related matters, so can you not exercise the same level of caution in matters of your lifetime partnership with your spouse? The worldly life is nothing but a factory and a museum of conflicts. Some household will have a few, some will have more and some will have a lot.

People do not know how to adjust in their homes but they sit down to read scriptures about the soul! You foolish people! Let go of this nonsense! First, learn to do this! You do not even know how to adjust at home. Such is the world! So, you must get your work done.

The *Gnani* Liberates You From The Worldly Web

Questioner : This worldly life accounts are nothing but a losing proposition, so then why do some appear profitable at times?

Dadashri : From whatever losses you incur, if you feel any of them as being beneficial, then you should deduct them, from your overall karmic account. This worldly life has come about as a result of many multiplications, so if you divide using the method I show you, there will be nothing left. If you learn from this, it is fine otherwise make a resolve of, 'I want to absolutely follow Dada's *Agnas* and I want to bring an end to all worldly conflicts.' The moment you make such a decision, you are on your way.

It has become increasingly difficult to pass the days. The husband comes home complaining of chest pains. The son comes home saying he failed the examination. She tells the son, "Your father has chest pains." She worries about him having a heart attack. Thoughts such as these will bombard you from all directions; they will not let you be at peace.

The *Gnani Purush* shows you a way to break free from the web of this worldly life. He shows you the path of liberation and what is more, He will put you on that path and you will have the experience that you have been liberated from the trap of all conflicts.

You Will Encounter The One Who Liberates With Such Intention!

Everything is under the control of some other authority. Eating, drinking, or getting your children married, are all beyond your control. All forms of conflicts are within you. These are the *kashayas*: anger, pride, attachment and greed. They control everything. When the *Gnani Purush* gives you the knowledge of the Self, you become free from the control of these *kashayas* and their entrapment. The nature of the worldly life is such that it will keep you bound, even if you want nothing to do with it. Therefore, keep an internal intent for liberation, *moksha*. You have had such a desire in your countless past lives but do you not need someone who can show you the way? You need a *Gnani Purush*, who knows and will show you the way.

When you have a band-aid on your arm, it is so sticky that it will not come off without pulling the hair on your arm. The worldly life is sticky, just like a band-aid; it will only come off when the *Gnani* shows you the medicine of how to take it off. This worldly life is not such that it will free you even if you wish to leave it. Anyone who relinquishes the worldly life is able to do so because of his past karma. Whether a person acquires a worldly life or a life of an ascetic, he has been able to do so because of his karma. It is only after you acquire the real vision, that you attain final liberation.

You are not the doer of anything. Anger, pride, deceit and greed; these *kashayas* run everything; they are the rulers. It is only when you realize the Self, that these *kashayas* leave. You may repent for an angry outburst, but the Lord has said that nothing can be gained if a person does not know how to do *pratikraman*. Knowing how to do *pratikramans* leads to liberation.

These *kashayas* will not leave you in peace even for a moment. You become engulfed in attachment when your son is getting married, at that time you are in complete oblivion. At other times, you experience so much inner turmoil. This is all relative and temporary. You are simply act out your role as you would in a drama. Once you leave this body, you will have to resume your role in a drama elsewhere. These relationships are not real; they are merely worldly relationships. Once the karmic account is finished, the son will not go with the parents.

Instead, you complain, "This man insulted me!" Let go of your foolishness, insults are meant to be swallowed. When your husband insults you, you should remember, 'This is my karmic account, my husband is merely an instrument in the process and that he is really innocent. When my karmas take a turn for the better, my husband will give me a lot of respect.' You must remain calm and try to resolve the matter, but if in your mind you think, 'I am not at fault and yet why does he speak to me this way?' then you will stay awake for hours at night, and finally tire and fall asleep.

Those who have become a superior over God have attained something, but those who have tried to become superiors over their wives have been doomed. The one who tries to become the superior will be doomed for sure. But what does God say? "If you become my superior, I will be happy. I have enjoyed being your superior for so long but now if you become my superior, it would be good."

The understanding that what the *Gnani* gives you will liberate you. What can you possibly achieve without the understanding? The religion of the *Vitarag* Lords will liberate you from all miseries.

At home, you should turn things around. The atmosphere in your home should be wonderful. A wife should feel as though she would never be able to find another husband like hers and the husband should feel as though he would never be able to find a wife like his. If you are able to bring about such changes, then truly you are worthy.

[6] Business with Principles

The Goal Of Life

Dadashri : Why do you conduct your business?

Questioner : To earn money.

Dadashri : Money for what?

Questioner : That I do not know.

Dadashri : Let me give you an analogy. A man runs an engine all day long, but for what? Nothing, he just lets the engine run idle. He does not use the energy from the engine; your situation is like that. What do you live life for? Just for earning money? Every living being is in search of happiness. Your life is meant for searching a path whereby you attain freedom from all miseries.

Think Constructively But Do Not Worry

Questioner : I have a lot of worries about my business. I am faced with a lot of difficulties.

Dadashri : Understand this much. Understand that the moment you start to have worries, your work is going to be ruined. If you do not worry a lot, then your work will not be ruined. Worries are obstructions towards any work or business. Worries will bring death to a business. The nature of a business is that it increases and decreases; it becomes full and then it empties. Discharge is inevitable after a charge in the relative realm. In all this, that is filling and emptying, nothing hurts or affects that which is your own, the Self. This is exact.

Are your wife, and children, your son and his wife, partners in your business?

Questioner : They help share in my happiness and my sorrow.

Dadashri : You are the guardian of your wife and your children. Why should the guardian be the only one to worry? Your family members tell you not to worry, and yet you do.

Questioner : What is the nature of worries? The worries are not present when we are born, so where do they come from?

Dadashri : As your intellect increases, so does your internal suffering. When a child is born, does he have intellect? It is necessary for you to think about your business for ten to fifteen minutes, but if you go beyond this, then you will be bombarded with thought after thought and that is going beyond normality. When that happens, you must let go. Thoughts about your business are inevitable but if you become engrossed with the thoughts, they will linger on, leading to worries, and such adverse meditation is very detrimental for you.

Keep Your Intentions Pure To Pay All Debts

Questioner : I have incurred a very heavy loss in my business, what should I do? Should I close the business? I am in deep debt.

Dadashri : Losses incurred in a cotton business, cannot be recouped by opening a grocery store. Losses incurred in business have to be regained from the same business; you cannot recoup your losses by doing a different job. Can you recoup losses from a business of contract by opening up a beetle nut store? The injuries you incurred from whatever trade you were in will have to be healed in the same trade. Therein lies the medicine for your wounds.

The only thing you have to maintain is that you do not want to hurt any living being, even in the slightest degree. Be pure in your intentions to pay off all your debts. If your intentions are pure, you will be able to fulfill all your financial obligations. Money is considered the eleventh life, and therefore you must never keep money that belongs to others. If others keep your money then it does not matter, but your intention must always be that you want to pay them back, down to the last penny. Keep this intention in your awareness, and then you can engage in your business. Play your game, but do not become a player. If you become a player, then you will be doomed! Do not speculate in your business.

Be Aware of the Dangers but Be Fearless

Every business has gains and losses associated with it. If there are a lot of mosquitoes in your room, they will not let you sleep. But, you would not be able to sleep even if there were only one or two. Therefore, you can say out loud, "Oh world of mosquitoes! Merely two mosquitoes will not let me sleep, so why don't the rest of you come also?" These profits and losses are like the mosquitoes.

What is the law? Avoid entering the depths of the ocean of business if possible. If you do, then do not be afraid. God is with you as long as you remain fearless. If you become afraid, God will say, "Go to Ohliya!" (muslim sage) or find a guru. There is no difference between a racecourse and a fabric store, as far as God is concerned. But if you want liberation, then it is better that you come out of this worldly ocean.

Do you know how I run my business? Before I set the ship of my business in the waters, I perform all the necessary religious rituals and then I whisper in the steamer's ear, "You may sink whenever you want to but that is not my wish." Then whether the steamer sinks after six months or after two years, I adjust to the situation and tell myself, 'At least it lasted six months.' Palaces of desires will not fail to bring disappointment. It is very difficult to remain detached in this worldly life, but you are able to do so because of the knowledge and the intellectual methods that I give to you.

Customers: Who Brings Them?

Questioner : I open my shop early and close late in order to attract more customers, is this right?

Dadashri : Who are you to attract customers? You should open your shop at the same time others do. If others open their shop at 7:00 a.m. and you open yours at 9:30 a.m., that is wrong. Close your shop at the same time others do. The worldly life tells you that you should observe what others do. You should sleep when others do. If you make noise till 2:00 in the morning, is that acceptable? Do you worry about how you are going to digest your food after you eat? The consequences of your eating become evident in the morning, without fail. This principle also applies to business everywhere.

Questioner : Dada, recently I have had no customers in the business, what should I do about that?

Dadashri : If you lose electricity and you sit there waiting and pondering, 'When will the light come back? When will the light come back?' will it come back sooner? What do you do in that situation?

Questioner : I notify the company or I will go there myself.

Dadashri : Do you not call the company hundred times?

Questioner : No.

Dadashri : When this light went off, we were all singing. Did the light not come back on its own?

Questioner : Does that mean we should remain detached?

Dadashri : It is wrong to remain detached, but it is also wrong to become attached. You just have to maintain from within, 'It would be good if the lights were to come back.' You are asked to remain calm. 'It would be good if the customers come.' Just maintain this much but do not get excited. Maintain regularity and do not spoil your inner intent. To maintain regularity is your true effort. Do not get agitated if there are no customers and when some day there is a throng of customers, see to it that every customer is served to their satisfaction. Instead, people get angry with their employees if there are no customers. How would you feel if you were in their shoes? The poor worker comes to do your job and you tell them off. He will put up with your abuse, but at the same time, he will bind vengeance against you. You should never be harsh to your servant. He is human too! The poor man is miserable at home, and at work, you keep telling him off. Where is the poor man to go? Show him some kindness.

When a customer comes to your shop, show him your goods with love and patience, and when you have no customers, then remember God and meditate. Instead, you fret looking to see if any customers are coming and your intellect then troubles you, 'Today I am going to make a loss'. You become overcome with anxiety and then you take out your frustrations on your workers. You become engulfed in adverse meditative states. Whatever customers come to your shop, they come because of *vyavasthit* and only those who are meant to come will come, so do not interfere in the process. When you have customers, you can haggle over the prices but you should not allow any *kashayas* (anger, pride, attachment and greed) to transpire, you have to accomplish your work by appeasing them. If your arm were to get trapped under a big rock, would you break the rock by hitting it with a hammer? No because that would crush your arm.

Instead, you would try to pry it out gently. If you use *kashayas* in your interactions, you will create vengeance and one vengeance will lead to endless vengeance. Vengeance is the basis of the world's existence; vengeance is the main cause.

Honesty – God's license.

Questioner : Today if a person tries to do business honestly, his business incurs a loss, why is that?

Dadashri : When you do your work honestly you will have to face only one difficulty, but when you work dishonestly then you will have to face two difficulties. You will be able to break free of the difficulty you have to face because of your honesty, but it will be very hard to become free from difficulties resulting from your dishonesty. Honesty is the biggest license (of approval) from God and no one will be able to harass that person. Are you having thoughts about destroying that license?

Why Delight and Sorrow In Profit and Loss?

If you do business with honesty, your profits will be 66,616 and if you do it with dishonesty it will be 66,616. Which would you chose?

I have a big business but whenever our business receives an official letter from the government, it is on the business, it is not on my head, because I associate both profit and loss to the business. I take home only the amount of money that I would make as a salaried employee. The remaining profit stays in the business account and so do the losses.

There is nothing to be gained in having anxieties about money. If you breathe a sigh of relief when you have some savings in the bank, then you will experience sorrow when that money goes away. There is nothing in this world worth depending upon, because everything is temporary.

Ideal Business And Its Limits

The best kind of business is one where there is no violence or harm against other living entity through the mind, speech and body. No one should get hurt from your business, but here grocers will sell their customers short; they will weigh the grains and then take some out. They have even learnt to adulterate their goods. A person who adulterates food for profit is doomed for the animal kingdom. Keep religious principles in your business otherwise degradation will set in.

Questioner : How much should a person expand his business?

Dadashri : Expand your business to the extent where it will let you sleep well at night. And when you want to do away with it, then you will be able to do so. And in the process do not invite unnecessary difficulties.

Interest On Money Loaned

Questioner : The scriptures prohibit one from charging interest.

Dadashri : Our scriptures have not raised an objection to interest but when a person's intentions turn towards interest then it becomes detrimental to him. There is no problem in you charging interest on your money as long as the other person is not hurt by it.

Be Noble in Your Frugality

How should you practice frugality in your home? You should practice it in a way that it does not offend anyone. You should never practice frugality in your kitchen or when it comes to sharing food. You should be generous in your frugality. If frugality enters your kitchen, it will ruin your mind and when you have visitors, you will think, 'The rice will be used up.' On the other hand, if a person is extravagant, I will tell him to practice noble frugality.

[7] Interaction With Subordinates And Employees

Protect the Subordinate

Questioner : Dada my boss works me very hard, he pays me very little, and he reprimands me all the time.

Dadashri : These Indian bosses will cheat their own wives but in the end, at the time of death he is the one who is cheated. Some of these bosses extract heavy work from their workers, they do not even let them have their meals peacefully; they do not pay enough wages. When the income tax officers cut into their profits then they will behave themselves, but these bosses of today do not pay their share of the taxes either.

People criticize and attack their subordinates. You fools! Why don't you attack your boss? That is where your victory counts! Such are the interactions of the world. The Lord has said, "Protect those who are under you." Those who have followed this principle have become Gods. I used to do this from my very childhood.

If a servant were to drop the tray of teacups, his boss will yell at him, "What's wrong with you? Are your hands broken? Can't you see?" That poor man is just a servant. In reality, the servant does not break anything; a wrong belief makes it appear that way. The breaker of the cups is someone else. When the innocent servant is accused of being the culprit, he will somehow get even, in some other life.

Questioner : So who is it that breaks the cups?

Dadashri : I disclose everything when I give *Gnan*.

Who breaks the glasses? Who runs the world? I will solve all those puzzles for you, at that time. What should you do in a situation like that? In the absence of having the right knowledge, what should you do? The servants are sincere; they will not break anything deliberately.

Questioner : No matter how sincere he is, if the cups break at his hands, is he not indirectly responsible?

Dadashri : Yes, he is responsible, but you should know the extent of his responsibility. First, you should ask him, "Are you all right? You did not get burnt, did you?" If he is scalded, you should apply some ointment on his burn. Later quietly tell him that from now on he should be careful.

Abuse of Power

Some with power and authority will oppress those under them. The one who abuses his power will lose it. He will also lose his right to be born as a human being again. If you reprimand a person for just one hour, you will bind one whole lifetime. It is a different matter if you reprimand a person who is your opponent.

Questioner : If the other person is difficult and adamant, should we not be the same?

Dadashri : You are not to see anything about the other person. He is responsible for his own actions. If some outlaws confronted you and you behaved like an outlaw too, then it is a different matter, but instead you just hand over your possessions to them, don't you? What is the point in acting boldly in front of the meek? What really counts is despite your strength; you become humble when dealing with the weak.

These officers come to work after getting into a fight with their wives and take it out on their workers. What fools! Be

nice to your assistants, what will become of you if your assistant
were to deceive you into signing certain important documents to
get even with you? You need your assistants.

I take very good care of my assistants because the
business runs smoothly on account of them.

Many people try to impress their boss to get into his
good books. If the boss says to charge twenty percent, he will
charge twenty-five percent to impress his boss! He is binding
demerit karma in the process.

[8] Nature's Guest

Nature is Helpful from the Moment One Is Born!

Every living being in this world is a guest of nature.
Nature brings to you everything, but because you do not
understand this fact, you remain restless internally and
externally, all day long. That is because you believe you are
the doer. That is all an illusion. In reality, no one is the doer
of anything.

Is everything not ready for you before you are born?
Does a baby have to worry about its milk after it is born? The
baby's milk and all its needs will be ready before its birth. The
doctor, the midwife and if a midwife is not available, the
barber's wife will be there for sure! Regardless, certain
preparations will fall into place and these preparations depend
upon the class; the status of the guest that is going to be born.
A first class guest will have first class preparations; a second-
class guest will have preparations suitable for a second-class
guest and a third class guest will have preparations suitable
according to his class. There will always be a category of
classes, will there not? All this is determined by one's karmas
from one's past life. You have come with all the preparations,
so why must you worry and bother others unnecessarily?

If you are a guest in someone's home, should you not behave as a guest, with humility? If I am a guest in your house, should I not be polite and mindful? If you tell me that I have to sleep in a certain place, do I not have to obey? If my lunch is served at 2:00 p.m., then I should eat quietly. I should eat whatever is served to me. I should not complain about the food, because I am a guest. Now how does it look if a guest goes into the kitchen and starts to cook? If as a guest, you interfere in household matters, who will allow you to stay? Eat whatever they put on your plate; if they serve you *basoondi* (dessert), just eat it. You cannot say, "I do not eat sweets." Eat leisurely, whatever they serve you. If you are not too fond of what they serve you, eat little, but eat you must! Be mindful of all the regulations a guest must comply with. The guest cannot do *raag-dwesh* (attachment-abhorrence). Can a guest do *raag-dwesh*? The guest always maintains his boundaries.

At home, I live like a guest. All my needs are met. Wherever you live as a guest, you should not trouble the host. Everything I need comes my way, all I have to do is think about it, and it comes. If things do not come my way, I have no problems. I am a guest of nature. If nature does not will something for you, know that it is in your best interest and when it does, that too is in your best interest. If things were in your control, what would happen if your beard were to grow only on half of your face? If the control were in your hands, you would make a mess of everything. The control is in the hands of nature. Nature never makes any mistakes. Everything is in exact order. Take your teeth for example, each have different functions. You have teeth for chewing, teeth for cutting, teeth for grinding. Just look at how wonderful everything is. Upon your birth, you are given the whole body, hands, feet, nose, ears, and eyes. You get everything. And when you put your hands in your mouth, you find no teeth! Did nature a mistake there? No.

Nature knows that a baby needs to drink milk the moment it is
born. Babies cannot digest any food except milk. The baby has
to drink its mother's milk and if the baby were to have teeth,
it would bite the mother! Just look at the wonder of nature's
arrangements. Teeth will begin to erupt, as the baby needs
them. First come the four front teeth, the rest come in gradually.
And in old age when the teeth are gone, no new ones will grow
in their place.

Nature gives protection from all sides; it takes care of
you as if you are a king. But what can anyone do when the
unfortunate foolish one not know how to live life?

The Precision of *Vyavasthit*

After an evening meal, you fall asleep and start snoring.
Why don't you investigate what goes on inside the body and
how it works? There you will say, "What can I do?" What is
nature? Nature is that you have digestive enzymes and juices
in the stomach for the digestion process. When you wake up
in the morning, the urine is in its place, the blood is where it
needs to be and the excrement is in its correct place. How
beautiful is this systematic arrangement of nature! Nature
performs a monumental task inside your body. If a doctor
were put in charge of a person's digestion, he will kill that
person. Nature has such perfect control over the production
of the digestive juices, that they will last till you die, whereas
if a doctor were given the responsibility over the digestive
juices, he will release too much one day and not enough the
next.

Nature has such beautiful play in its hands and in your
hands, you have your business, but truly speaking it is not in
your hands; you do not have control over it, you simply believe
you do and consequently you fret and worry needlessly. Sitting
in a taxi from Dadar to Central, the passenger develops

anxieties and suffers upon the thoughts, 'What if there is an accident?' No one is going to crash with you. All you have to do is to exercise reasonable caution and proceed, in all matters of life. Your only responsibility is to look in front and walk, that is all. In reality, even that is not your responsibility. Nature will make you do even that. But instead, people are not only inattentive to what is ahead of them, they interfere in the process, exercise their ego, 'I am doing all this.' Nature is beautiful. If within you there runs a factory, which is so complex, don't you think that everything on the outside will run smoothly also? Nothing on the outside needs to be controlled. What do you think needs to be controlled?

Questioner : If someone does something wrong, that too is not under his control?

Dadashri : No, he does not have control. And he cannot make it go wrong either. It is because his intentions were wrong in his past life, that today he has done wrong. He had interfered in the workings of nature in the past life. Just observe the animals around you, the crows, the dogs, cats etc. They do not have hospitals or legal courts and yet do they not resolve their conflicts? When two bulls fight, they fight a lot but after they separate, do they go looking for a court? If you see them the next day, they are both roaming around leisurely. But the foolish human beings have courts and hospitals and even then they are constantly unhappy. They are always complaining. What can you call these people? Just look at how attractive the sparrows, the cat, and the dogs look. They do not take any special herbal concoctions during the winter and look at what humans do in cold climate. They take all kinds of concoctions, and even then, they look so unattractive and ugly. Because of the ego, even the most beautiful person appears ugly. Therefore, there must be some mistake somewhere. Should one not think about this?

Nature Still Comes To Your Aid

Questioner : I have thoughts that are virtuous but they do not last. Then the evil thoughts come. What is this?

Dadashri : What are thoughts? Thoughts will work when you want to make progress or even when you want to regress. You take the godly path and then you turn back. It's like that. You go forward one mile and then you turn back one mile; one mile forward and one mile backward. It is better to keep thoughts of just one kind. If you are going to go backwards, keep going backwards and if you are going to go forward, keep going forward. Nature will help the one who wants to go forward and also the one who wants to go backwards. Nature says, "I will help you in anything you want to do. If you want to steal, I will help you even then." There is tremendous help from nature and it is through this help that everything in the world functions. But you are the one who cannot decide what you want. Nature is ready to help you if you decide what you want. First decide what you want and then every morning, recall your decision with determination. You should remain sincere to your determination; then nature will side with you and help you. You are the guest of nature.

So understand this fact. Nature says, "I will help you." God does not help, God does not have the time. Everything around us is the creation of nature and the creation only takes place because of the presence of God.

Questioner : Are we nature's guest or are we part of nature?

Dadashri : We are part of nature as well as a guest of nature. To live as a guest is our preference. Wherever you sit you will get air and water, free of cost. The priceless commodity of nature is free to you. That which nature values are the very thing humans do not. That which nature does not value, like diamonds and gold, humans value too much.

[9] Human Values

Sincerity and Morality

Sincerity and morality are the two basements (foundations) of this world. If these two values rot away, everything will collapse. The greatest of wealth in this era is sincerity and morality. At one point in Hindustan these two values were in abundance, but now people of Hindustan have exported them to foreign countries and do you know what they have imported in return? Etiquette! People have now become possessed with demons of etiquette. That is why they have become restless. What need do we have for etiquette? Etiquette is for those who lack inner beauty and radiance. We have within us the inner beauty and radiance of the *Tirthankar* Lords. We are the progeny and descendants of great *maha rishis*. Even if you have only rags to wear, your own radiance and aura will speak for who you are.

Questioner : Can you explain the exact meanings of sincerity and morality?

Dadashri : Morality means to enjoy whatever is yours by right and that which comes to you naturally. This is the ultimate definition of morality. Morality is very profound; volumes of scriptures have been written on this subject, but you should understand it by this ultimate definition.

Sincerity: the person who is not sincere to others is not sincere to himself. You should not be insincere to anyone in the slightest; you break your own sincerity when you do.

If in this day and age, you possess both morality and sincerity, it is more than enough. Even if you have one of these two qualities, it will liberate you completely. You must however, adhere to it, and whenever you have problems in life, you can come to the *Gnani* and clear up any issues about what is moral or immoral.

The multiplication of the *Gnani's* grace and your sincerity will make you successful in all of life's endeavors.

Liberation Even Through Insincerity

If a man with twenty percent sincerity and eighty percent insincerity were to come to me and say, "I want liberation but what should I do with this baggage that I have?" I would tell him to become one hundred percent insincere and then I would show him some other method that will liberate him. This eighty percent debt may take forever to pay off, instead become bankrupt just once. You can achieve liberation if you hold on to even just one of Dada's sentences. I do not have any problem if you have been insincere with the entire world but if you were to remain sincere here, to Dada, then you can attain liberation. Complete insincerity is also a great quality; it can take you to *moksha*, because you have completely turned against God and God has no choice but to take even his opponent to *moksha*. Either a devotee of God goes to *moksha* or a complete opponent of God goes to *moksha*. Therefore I tell a person who is ruined to become one hundred percent insincere. Then I show him another path that will take him all the way to *moksha*. I have to also give him a solution; he cannot win by being insincere only.

[10] Ideal Interactions

Ultimately You Will Need Ideal Interactions with the World

No one has achieved liberation without having ideal worldly interactions. The Jain's worldly interaction (*vyavahar*) is not ideal. Vaishnav worldly interaction is not ideal. Ideal interaction is required to attain *moksha*.

Ideal interaction means no living being gets hurt even in the slightest degree. It means that you do not hurt your family, your neighbors or anyone else.

It is not worth insisting on the Jain or the Vaishnav way of life because their way of life is not ideal. Lord Mahavir's interactions were ideal. Ideal interaction is the one that will not hurt or offend even an enemy; it is a sign of approaching liberation. Liberation is not attainable by being a Jain or a Vaishnav. My *Agnas* (five Cardinal principles of *Gnan* given after Self-Realization) will ensure ideal interactions. My *Agnas* will help you maintain equanimity during any physical and or metal suffering and suffering instilled upon you by others. Elsewhere, all interactions are relative, but this is a science. Science means real.

In ideal interactions, you must hurt no one. That is all you have to focus on and if your actions do hurt someone, you should immediately do *pratikraman*. You cannot interact with them in the manner in which they interact with you. I am not referring to the business transactions and the exchange of money; those are all routine worldly dealings, and that is not what I am referring to when I talk about interactions. You should only be concerned with maintaining awareness that you hurt no one and if you do, then do *pratikraman* immediately. That is considered ideal interactions.

Mine is an ideal *vyavahar*; ideal worldly interaction. It will never happen that anyone will have any problems on my account. If someone causes problems for me and I do the same to him, then what is the difference between him and I? I am straightforward, without any interfering intellect. I knowingly allow people to deceive me. The other person thinks, 'Dada is still naive.' Yes it is better to be naive and escape than to be smart and get caught in his prison (karmic consequences). One day my partner told me, "You are very naive." I replied, "Naive is the one who thinks I am naive." "But so many people cheat you," he argued. So I told him, "I allow them to cheat me on purpose."

My interactions are completely ideal. If there is even a slightest weakness in a person's interactions, he is not considered completely worthy of liberation.

Questioner : Is there any partiality in the *Gnani's* interactions between two people?

Dadashri : There is never any prejudice or bias in the way the *Gnani* sees things. There is *vitaragata* in my vision; I see them only as pure Souls. There is difference in the way I interact with them. If a wealthy businessman were to come here with his chauffer, and I made the businessman sit across from me and ask the driver to sit beside me, it would infuriate the businessman. That is not ideal interaction. And if the President were to come, I would get up and welcome him. I cannot dismiss the appropriate interactions needed towards him. I would seat him higher, out of respect. If he is interested in acquiring *Gnan* from me, then I would seat him down on the floor, otherwise I would ask him to sit on a chair. That which is commonly acceptable to people, is referred to as *'vyavahar'* and that which is acceptable for liberation is called *'nischaya'*. Therefore you have to accept the *vyavahar* suitable to people, as *vyavahar*. If I do not get up to welcome the President, he will feel hurt and I become responsible for that.

Questioner : Should we revere those who are bigger than us?

Dadashri : Bigger does not necessarily mean older in

age. Nevertheless if you interact with the elderly, then you have to respect them and those who have advanced in their knowledge, should be revered too.

You must go home on time from *satsang*. How does it look if you knock on the door at midnight? People at home may tell you to come home whenever you like, but their mind will not leave them alone. The mind will show them all kinds of things. How can you hurt them at all? These are all laws and rules and you have to abide by.

If you get up at two o'clock in the morning and pray to the Soul, is anyone likely to say anything? No they will not.

Pure Interactions: Right interactions

Questioner : What is *shuddha vyavahar* (pure interaction) and *sada vyavahar* (right interaction)?

Dadashri : Pure interaction begins only after Self-Realization and until then it is considered right interaction, *sada vyavahar.*

Questioner : What is the difference between the two?

Dadashri : Right interaction is associated with the ego. Pure interaction is egoless; it is without any ego. Pure interaction gives you complete *dharma dhyana,* absence of negative meditative states of *arta* and *raudra dhayana* and right interaction gives you only a small fraction of *dharma dhyana.*

As long as there is pure interaction, there is also *shuddha upyog*, (i.e. pure awareness). Pure awareness means that You (the Self) remain the Knower and the Observer, of the pure interaction.

Krupadudev has said, "Collective sectarian opinions and imagination are not right worldly interactions."

In all religious sects there is talk about the real but it is only imaginary real. When they do not even have the right interaction, how can there ever be pure interaction there? Pure interaction is the egoless state. Pure interaction is devoid of competition. If you enter a competition then you will create *raag-dwesh* (attachment-abhorrence). I tell everyone they are fine where they are but if they feel there is something missing, then they can come to me. Here the only thing you get is love. If someone comes here with a lot of abhorrence, we still give him love.

Kramic, the traditional religious path, means that first you have to purify your worldly interactions and then you become the pure Self. In the *Akram* path you become the pure Self first and then you make your interactions pure. In pure interaction, there may be interaction of every kind, but there is no attachment in it. Pure interaction begins one or two life times prior to one's final liberation.

Nischaya, the state of the Self, is unaffected by interactions. Where no interactions touch or influence, is *nischaya*. Fulfill all of your worldly interactions to the point where they do not affect *nischaya*, regardless of what their interaction may be.

There is a difference between a clear, right interaction and pure interaction. That which keeps an interaction good is called *manavdharma* (religion of man) and pure interaction takes you to *moksha*. When you do not quarrel at home or outside, it is considered good interaction. What is an ideal interaction? It is one, which spreads the aura of the worldly self.

Once you attain ideal interaction and the state of the pure Self, what more is there to do? Just this much can change the whole universe.

Ideal interactions link with Liberation

Dadashri : What kind of interactions do you want?

Questioner : Absolutely ideal.

Dadashri : What is the point in having ideal interactions when you become old? Your interactions should be ideal from the beginning of your life.

If there is only one person with ideal interaction in this world then it is possible for him to change the whole world.

Questioner : How can we achieve ideal interaction?

Dadashri : By remaining in the state of the Self, which you all *mahatmas* have received, will bring about ideal interactions automatically. In this state, no interference of any kind can occur. If you experience any interference, then it means you are not abiding by my *Agnas*. The five *agnas* I give you are capable of keeping you in the same state as the state of Lord Mahavir. My *Aganas* are not restrictive or obstructive in your interactions. They help maintain your ideal interaction. This *Gnan* can make your interactions completely ideal. Who achieves liberation? It is the one with ideal interactions. Dada's *Agnas* bring forth ideal interaction. It is not ideal interaction if a slightest mistake occurs. Liberation is not some figment of the imagination. It is real; it is a fact. It is not something someone has invented.

I met a man in a very prominent *ashram*. I asked him what he was doing there. He told me he had been living there for ten years. I informed him that back home in his village his parents were slowly dying from poverty and old age. He said, "So what can I do about that? If I try to help them, then my work and duty of my religion suffers." How can you call this a duty of religion? Religion is when you take care of your parents, brothers, and others. Your conduct should be ideal. How can any conduct or interaction that shows contempt towards your duties, your parents etc., be considered your religion?

It is also a terrible mistake to curse anyone, even in your mind. Equally deleterious are actions carried out in secrecy. A person may think to himself, 'No one will know,' or 'Who is going to find out?' You fools! This world is not haphazard by any means; it is not without laws. These are terrible and grave mistakes and these very mistakes are the causes of suffering.

Your interactions should be ideal. *Kashayas* will arise if you become small-minded in your interactions. This life is like a tiny boat. Enjoy as much of it as you can while you are in it, but realize that with this boat, you have to get to the other shore.

Therefore understand what I am saying. You only have to understand what the *Gnani Purush* says. You do not have to do anything. Having acquired the understanding, the one who conforms becomes a *vitarag*.

Jai Sat Chit Anand